Jill Carter works as a natural health practitioner in Somerset. She is a State Registered Nurse and practises healing, therapeutic massage, acupressure and aromatherapy, and offers dietary and nutritional counselling.

Alison Edwards set up the Polden Naturopathic Centre in Somerset over 20 years ago. She is a State Registered Nurse and a practitioner of complementary medicine, and acts as consultant to clinics throughout Britain and overseas.

by the same authors
The Elimination Diet Cookbook

A Note to the Reader
The information contained in this book is given for the
purposes of helping people who wish to use and learn more
about a rotation diet. Before following the advice, the reader
is advised to give careful consideration to the nature of their
problem and to consult a healthcare practitioner if in any
doubt. This book should not be used as a substitute for
medical treatment and whilst every care has been taken to
ensure the accuracy of the information, the authors and
publishers cannot accept any responsibility for any problems
arising out of experimentation with the method described.

The Rotation Diet Cookbook

A 4-Day Plan for Relieving Allergies

Jill Carter and Alison Edwards

ELEMENT

Shaftesbury, Dorset ● Rockport, Massachusetts
Brisbane, Queensland

© Element Books Ltd 1997
Text © Jill Carter and Alison Edwards 1997

First published in Great Britain in 1997 by
Element Books Limited
Shaftesbury, Dorset SP7 8BP

Published in the USA in 1997 by
Element Books, Inc.
PO Box 830, Rockport, MA 01966

Published in Australia in 1997 by
Element Books Limited
for Jacaranda Wiley Limited
33 Park Road, Milton, Brisbane 4064

Cover design by Bridgewater Book Company
Text illustrations by Mary Stubberfield
Designed and typeset by Linda Reed and Joss Nizan
Printed and bound in J W Arrowsmith Ltd
Bristol, Avon

British Library Cataloguing in Publication
data available

Library of Congress Cataloging in Publication
data available

ISBN 1–85230–965–2

Contents

Introduction

Life is a ceaseless movement of rotation and change. The earth rotates and the seasons change and yet we tend to eat the same foods day in, day out. Do you, for example, eat toast for breakfast, sandwiches for lunch and pasta in the evening? Or do you reach for that welcome cup of coffee at regular intervals throughout the day? If so, you may need to consider the effect this is having on your body.

If a food is eaten too frequently, the body is unable to break it down and process it completely and can therefore become overloaded. If you are already allergic or intolerant to foods, you will probably then become allergic to even more things. Even if you don't suffer from allergies, it is likely that you will feel the effects of the overload.

The Rotation Diet offers a way of spacing foods so that you can recover from the effects of a food before it is eaten again. The diet was originally designed to help people who are allergic to foods, but it can be wonderfully beneficial for anyone. Many people with highly demanding lifestyles find that their energy levels increase and that they feel much better when they rotate their foods. After all, it was not so long ago that we depended on food grown close at hand, and the seasons of the year dictated a natural rotation.

If you have discovered that you are allergic to certain foods, either from following the Elimination Diet laid out in *The Elimination Diet Cookbook*, or from the many tests available, it is important that you should understand how to plan and use the Rotation Diet. However, the prospect of embarking on a rotation diet can be so daunting that all but the most determined either give up in the early stages or not even start at all. It is for this reason that this book has been written. This book will give you a clear understanding of the principles involved and show you just how to follow them. Once these principles have been grasped, the diet can then be adapted to your individual needs. In this book, you will find delicious recipes varying from the very simple to the more elaborate; you will also find advice about other therapies that can help you overcome your allergy problem.

It may not be by chance that you have turned the cover of this book or that the title has caught your eye. Hopefully there will be something here which will help you or your child, spouse or close friend to improve the quality of your lives and to achieve full health.

Daphne (eight-years old) was constantly away from school due to persistent headaches, diarrhoea and tummy aches. She was referred to her local hospital and after counselling treatment failed, she was referred to a dietician who put her on a milk-, egg-, beef- and poultry-free diet. When this did not help, she was advised to stop eating anything containing preservatives. Her mother then found a natural medicine centre and a test revealed reactions to wheat, oats, barley and rye. Because there had been a long history of illness, a rotation diet was recommended. Milk, eggs, beef and poultry were returned to the diet in rotation, but the cereal grains were strictly avoided. Her mother wrote a report stating 'no headaches and tummy aches; no time away from school; she attends willingly and happily every day and her general complexion is now pink and healthy rather than the black eyes and a white face. She has had no diarrhoea for eight weeks'.

Simon was a very quiet and introverted boy. He got good marks throughout his time at school and was given a place at Cambridge University to study chemistry. At the end of his second year, however, he had a breakdown and was diagnosed as having schizophrenia. For four years he was treated with various drugs and was unable to study. His parents then read about elimination and rotation diets in an American book about treating serious breakdowns. They were unable to find a practitioner to help them and it took them a few years to implement the system fully. Gradually his drugs were reduced, he could study again and he returned to Cambridge.

CHAPTER 1

An Explanation of Allergies and the Rotation Diet

It is useful to understand exactly what is meant by the term 'allergy'. The word allergy is derived from two Greek words: *allos* meaning 'other' and *ergon* interpreted to mean 'altered reaction'. It describes how the body may react to a normally harmless substance, such as a food, house dust, pollen or animal fur. This substance is then known as an allergen. The response may be immediate and very noticeable. Hives, skin rashes, puffy eyes, asthma attacks, vomiting, runny nose, joint stiffness and, in extreme cases, an anaphylactic shock may occur within seconds. This is a true allergy, well-recognized by doctors, and can be confirmed by a laboratory test.

However, the word 'allergy' has also become a catchword for what is really an intolerance or hidden allergy. This is much more common than a true allergy, but also more difficult to detect because the symptoms are more likely to occur hours or even days after contact with the offending substance. Although orthodox medicine now acknowledges the existence of food intolerances, it is unclear about the mechanism involved and laboratory tests are unable to give any confirmation.

All manner of symptoms may result from a food intolerance, ranging from headaches and migraine, chronic fatigue, fluctuating weight, digestive problems, pains in the neck and joints, muscular pains, arthritis, asthma, eczema, poor concentration and dizziness, to mood swings, emotional outbursts and even violent behaviour. In addition it has been found that food intolerances can play a part in many chronic conditions such as ME, AIDS and cancer, due to the depletion of the immune system.

The symptoms can also change. An elderly woman suffering from arthritis, for example, may have had constant feeding problems, windy colicky pains, constipation and teething troubles in early childhood. She may have suffered from eczema, hay fever, catarrh, repeated coughs, colds and ear infections, and was perhaps hyperactive and had learning and co-ordination difficulties at school. Later on in her life, she may have suffered from migraines, headaches, asthma, acne and depression. She may also have been affected by hormonal changes, particularly at puberty, during pregnancy, post-natally or during the menopause. This would have given rise to PMT, heavy or irregular periods, early morning sickness during pregnancy and post-natal and menopausal depression.

It is not known how an allergy or intolerance develops, but is seems that alterations in the Western lifestyle and diet during the last century, such as the refining of foods, changes in infant feeding and medical care, food additives, pesticides, the increased use of chemicals, atmospheric pollution and the stresses of modern society, have all played a part. Allergies and intolerances are now affecting a huge number of people and the number is increasing rapidly.

Detecting allergies and food intolerances can be complicated but you will no doubt have most, if not all, of the answers, if you have already followed an elimination diet. Alternatively, you may have had your allergies or food intolerances tested at a natural health clinic. In this case it is worth bearing in mind that 'allergy tests' are not always accurate and that allergies and intolerances can change over time. A period of general ill-health, a virus infection or any increased stress in your life can lead to an increase of allergic responses. Furthermore, assessing your own problems will give you more control over your body. So you may decide that you want to follow an elimination diet before embarking on the Rotation Diet. If this is the case, *The Elimination Diet Cookbook* will show you exactly how to do this as well as providing you with delicious recipes for each day.

The Rotation Diet

Having established which foods you are reacting to, it is helpful to follow a rotation diet. The purpose of a rotation diet is to prevent the development of new allergies and intolerances to foods. Often people find that if they avoid the foods to which they are allergic or intolerant, they experience a great improvement in their health initially but can then start to feel unwell again. This is because they have become allergic or intolerant to something else in the meantime – often a substitute food which they have eaten too frequently. For example, it is common for someone to replace cows' milk with soya milk, only to find that they then develop an intolerance to soya. In addition, a rotation diet can also reduce existing food allergies and intolerances as it allows the body to process each food properly. Hence it is a way for many people to overcome their intolerances and, for those with multiple food allergies and intolerances, it can often mean that they can include more items in their diet than they may otherwise be able to do.

The Rotation Diet plan

On average, it takes three days for a meal to pass through the human digestive system and to be processed by the body, so, to be safe, the diet is based on a four-day plan. For example, if you were to eat wheat on Monday, you would then not have it again until Thursday.

When foods are rotated, it is the whole food family to which the particular food belongs that is rotated. (A list of food families can be found at the end of this chapter.) This is important because people can also react to the 'relatives' of a food to which they are intolerant. For instance, if you are intolerant to onion, you may also react to leeks, garlic, chives and possibly asparagus. There are exceptions, though, particularly with the grass family which, as you will see in the plan, is rotated differently. This is because many people react only to wheat or corn, the most commonly-eaten members of the grass family, or only to the cereals which contain gluten or gluten-related substances, namely wheat, rye, barley and oats. Other likely exceptions include soya and peanuts which, although they belong to the pea family, may produce individual reactions.

You will need to avoid foods that you know cause reactions. The recipes have been designed to make it easy for you to leave out any of the foods that you cannot tolerate and perhaps substitute other foods that you can. You may also find that as your body clears, small sensitivities that had previously been masked, may appear. In this case, you will need to avoid these foods as well.

However, if you have multiple allergies or intolerances and therefore have a very limited diet, you may have to eat some of the foods which cause the least reactions. If so, it is best to limit these to just once in the particular day. Alternatively, you may find you can tolerate some foods if eaten less frequently; once in eight days, for example.

As the weeks go by and you feel your health improving, you could try to introduce a suspect food into your diet plan. It may very well be that as your body clears, so do your allergies and food intolerances. It is likely then, that foods to which you previously reacted may no longer cause you any problems. If this is so, you can then simply incorporate the food into your rotation diet. As long as you continue to rotate those foods, you should find that they will remain safe for you to eat.

This diet, therefore, may seem slightly tricky at first but the benefits are numerous and long-lasting. It *is* possible to recover your health from an allergy or food intolerance problem and a rotation diet should prove to be an important part of such a recovery.

Adapting the diet to your needs

A rotation diet is usually followed for several months, and for some it becomes a way of life. During this time, you may want to alter the diet and you will also need to consider what to do when away from home, eating out in restaurants, with friends or when travelling.

Making changes in your diet at home

Once you have mastered the principles, you may want to rearrange some of the food families. If, for example, you wanted to make a chicken and mushroom pie, you could move the mushrooms from Day 1 to Day 3. You would do this simply by avoiding mushrooms on Day 1 and then having them on Day 3. You would then need to wait at least three more days before you could eat them again. If you wanted to move them back to Day 1, you would need to avoid them on the following Day 1 and reintroduce them on the subsequent Day 1. If you then wanted to switch avocado from Day 2 to Day 4 you would need to remember that cinnamon and bay leaves belong to the same family as avocado. So you would have to wait until Day 4 before you could eat any of them.

Eating out and away from home

If you work full-time or travel around a lot, this diet should prove to be easy to follow as long as you are prepared. If you make your meals the night before or in the morning, you can then simply pack them into a container and take them with you. There is a general tendency to think of sandwiches when it comes to packed lunches. However, that means missing out on all the other things that could go into a lunch box. Many of the meat dishes and nut roasts are delicious cold, and you can make up rice or millet salads with plenty of raw vegetables, nuts and seeds. A thermos of soup is also a good idea.

We are all social beings and it is important that you do not curtail social engagements because of your new diet. Likewise, it may be tempting to abandon your regime in order to conform with everyone else. It is simply not worth it. As your health improves, you will notice your confidence increases as well and you will cease to waste time and energy worrying about what others may think.

Eating in restaurants is not usually too much of a trouble. If you know what you are looking for, then you can usually find sufficient for your needs. You can ask for the meat or fish without the sauce, for example, and fresh fruit for dessert. Try to resist fried food as the oil will have been overheated and usually reused. As for drinks, there is always mineral water.

Do not be afraid to ask for something different; chefs are often only too willing to oblige.

If you are travelling by plane, airlines will provide special diets without any problem if you remember to state what you want (within reason) at the time of booking your ticket.

Dinner parties could prove a little more awkward but only if you let them. You can tell your host at the time of the invitation that you are following a new diet and you are avoiding certain foods. If this is a problem you can simply offer to take your own food.

Easing symptoms

If, for whatever reason, you find that you have eaten something to which you react, you can ease symptoms with the following :

- One teaspoon of bicarbonate of soda and half a teaspoon of potassium bicarbonate dissolved in a glass of water. Potassium bicarbonate is not so easy to obtain but some chemists may be able to supply you.
- Vitamin C can also be very effective. Take 1–2g with a glass of water.
- You may wish to use a herbal alternative. Meadowsweet can be made up as an infusion by steeping 25g (1oz; ¼ cup) of the herb in ½ litre (1 pint; 2 cups) of boiling water. Strain and use in doses of 75ml (½ cup).
- Drinking plenty of water will also help as it will help flush the system.

If you have the occasional lapse with the rotation of foods you can always make adjustments and get back to your routine. It is important to go about the diet as naturally and as calmly as you can. Try not to become obsessed or too fanatical as this will lead to a situation where the diet is controlling you rather than you being in charge of it.

Removing chemicals

When following this diet and endeavouring to improve your health, you may find that you need to reduce the number of chemicals you are exposed to. Examples of these are strong-smelling or highly perfumed products such as dry cleaning fumes, harsh detergents, biological washing powders, fabric conditioners, shoe polish, household cleaning products such as artificial air fresheners, cosmetic aerosols and sprays, such as deodorants, hair sprays and perfume. Bars of pure soap and soap flakes are good alternatives for washing clothes, and domestic borax, soda crystals or vinegar and water can be used for household cleaning. Sodium bicarbonate can be used as a deodorant and pure alcohol instead of aftershave lotion. Be wary of foam-backed carpets and vinyl wallpapers, car fumes and gas. It is also important, of course, to avoid smoking, alcohol, unnecessary medications or recreational drugs. Toothpaste is another item to be careful of; sugar-free types are now widely available.

Do not be put off by the thought of having to change your daily life. Simply go about the alterations methodically and positively. Once you have bought the necessary items for your larder and store cupboard and eliminated the things that need to be eliminated, you can then just incorporate the changes into your routine. The difference this can make to your health and to your life can be wonderful.

> Sandra was always in trouble at school. She fell asleep over her desk, never did her homework and frequently arrived late. Her school demanded that Sandra see a psychologist who suggested that she was taking 'social' drugs. Her parents knew this was not so, however, and decided to check for allergies instead. Sandra was found to be reacting to milk produce, corn, potato, tomato, tea and particularly car fumes. Steps were taken to deal with all this and Sandra never fell asleep at school again.

Jim had suffered from fatigue, which at times turned into complete exhaustion, since the age of nine. He had been an athlete in his school team but when he became unable to walk very far, he had to leave the team. He then found he could not concentrate and was unable to do his school work. He felt continually ill as if he had a viral illness. The doctor thought he was depressed and at one point recommended he should leave home and attend a psychiatric centre. His parents did not agree with this diagnosis and kept Jim at home. They then heard about the work of clinical ecologists in America and they visited a clinic in New York. The advice given was to follow an elimination diet. A lot of vitamin and mineral supplements were also recommended as well as amino acids, enzymes and glandular substances. The family started on the diet and by Day 5 Jim felt much better. He gradually became stronger and began to be able to concentrate. Over the next few months there were several relapses. The family discovered a clinic using clinical ecological methods in England. Each time he relapsed, more foods were found to be causing symptoms. The family were then taught how to plan a rotation diet so that no food was eaten too frequently. This solved a lot of the problems and Jim was able to study again. In 1989 Jim finished a university degree. During his four years of study he cooked his own food and kept to a rotation diet. He attended social functions taking his food with him, and then went on to full-time work. Jim realizes that without a knowledge of rotation diets he might still be getting the wrong diagnoses and treatment, and he doubts if he would ever have completed his education.

The Food Family Chart

Amaranthacea   Amaranth.

Apple   Apple, pear, quince, loquat, pectin, cider.

Arum   Dasheen, eddoes.

Aster   Lettuce, chicory, endive, globe and Jerusalem artichoke, dandelion, sunflower, salsify, tarragon, curry leaves, camomile, yarrow, safflower oil.

Banana   Banana, plantain, arrowroot.

Beech   Chestnuts.

Beef   Beef, veal, all milk products: lamb/mutton, goat and milk products

Beet   Sugar beet, spinach, Swiss chard, beetroot.

Birch   Filberts, hazelnuts, birch oil (wintergreen)

Bird   All foul and game birds, including chicken, turkey, duck, goose, pigeon, quail, pheasant, partridge, grouse, eggs.

Blueberry   Blueberry, cranberry.

Buckwheat   Buckwheat, rhubarb, sorrel.

Caper   Capers.

Cashew   Cashew, pistachio, mango.

Citrus   Lemon, orange, grapefruit, lime, tangerine, citron.

Conifer   Juniper, pine nuts.

Crustacean   Crab, crayfish, lobster, prawn, shrimp.

Custard apple   Pawpaw, custard apple.

Cyperacea   Tiger nuts.

Deer   Venison.

Dillenia   Kiwi fruit (Chinese gooseberry).

Elder   Elderberry.

Flax   Linseed (flax).

Freshwater fish   Salmon, trout, pike, perch, bass.

Fungus   Mushrooms, yeast.

Ginger   East Indian arrowroot, ginger, cardamom, turmeric.

Gooseberry   Currant, gooseberry.

Grape   Grapes, raisins, sultanas, cream of tartar, wine.

Grass   Wheat, spelt wheat, corn (maize), oats, barley, rye, rice, wild rice, malt, millet, quinoa, bamboo shoots, sugar cane, sorghum, kamut.

Horsetail   Equisetum tea.

Laurel   Avocado, cinnamon, bay leaves.

Lily   Onion, garlic, asparagus, chives, leeks.

Madder   Coffee.

Mallow   Okra, hibiscus.

Maple   Maple syrup.

Melon   Watermelon, cantaloupe and other melons, cucumber, zucchini, marrow, pumpkin, acorn squash and other squashes.

Mint   Apple mint, basil, bergamot, hyssop, lavender, lemon balm, marjoram, oregano, peppermint, rosemary, sage, spearmint, savory, thyme.

Mollusc   Abalone, snail, squid, clam, mussel, oyster, scallop, octopus.

Moraceae   Hempseed.

Morning glory   Sweet potato.

Mulberry   Figs, mulberry, hops, breadfruit.

Mustard   Turnip, radish, horseradish, Chinese leaves, watercress, mustard and cress, cabbage, cauliflower, broccoli, Brussels sprouts, kohlrabi, kale, mustard seed, rape seed, daikon.

Myrtle   Allspice, cloves, guava.

Nutmeg   Nutmeg, mace.

Orchid   Vanilla.

Olive   Black or green olives.

Palm   Coconut, date, date sugar, sago.

Papaya   Papaya.

Parsley   Carrots, parsnips, celery, celeriac, fennel, anise, parsley, caraway, lovage, chervil, coriander, cumin, dill.

Passifloracea Passion fruit.

Pea Pea, sugar peas, mangetout, green beans, broad beans, dried beans (*aduki beans, black beans, black-eyed beans, butter beans, cannellini beans, chickpeas, flageolet beans, haricot beans, lima beans, mung beans, dried peas, split green peas, split yellow peas, pinto beans, red kidney beans, soya beans*), lentils (*brown lentils, continental lentils, puy lentils, split red lentils*), alfalfa sprouts, liquorice, peanuts, fenugreek, red clover, senna, carob, Rooibosch tea.

Pedalium Sesame seeds.

Pepper Black and white pepper, peppercorn.

Pineapple Pineapple.

Plum Plum, damson, cherry, peach, apricot, nectarine, prune, almond.

Poppy Poppy seed.

Potato Potato, tomato, aubergine (eggplant), peppers (capsicum), paprika, cayenne, tobacco.

Proteaceae Macadamia nuts.

Rose Strawberry, raspberry, blackberry, loganberry, rosehip.

Saltwater Fish Tuna, mackerel, herring, eel, halibut, turbot, anchovy, sardine and pilchard, whitebait, sprats, sea bass, plaice, sole, cod, hake, haddock, sea bream, mullet.

Soapberry Lychees.

Spurge Cassava (tapioca).

Star fruit Star fruit.

Subucaya Brazil nut.

Sterculia Cocoa.

Swine All pork products.

Tea Tea, green leaf.

Walnut Walnut, hickory nut, butternut, walnut, pecan.

Water chestnut Water chestnut.

Yam Yam.

CHAPTER 2

Preparing for your Diet

Setting up your kitchen

If you are new to cooking you may find the following utensils helpful.

- For chopping, cutting etc, you need a good set of knives – a small sharp vegetable knife, a serrated knife, a bread knife and a general purpose knife for meat, fish etc; two chopping boards of durable hardwood – one for meat and one for vegetables; a 'vegetable-only' scrubbing brush; a sturdy grater; a potato peeler; a strong stainless-steel sieve; a pestle and mortar for grinding nuts, seeds and spices; a lemon squeezer; a salad spinner to dry lettuce and leafy greens; a meat mincer (inexpensive, dual-purpose mincers are available which can also be used for making your own pasta); a burger press; a zester – for the peel on citrus fruits; a pair of kitchen scissors; a garlic press; a selection of spatulas; a colander.
- Cooking pots – the heavy enamelled or cast-iron saucepans and casserole dishes are good for the distribution of heat so that lower temperatures can be used. Alternatively, you may choose stainless-steel or glass, but do avoid aluminium, copper and non-stick varieties. If you are buying a wok, choose the oriental type which has been designed for low-fat and fat-free cooking. It is also worth investing in a stainless-steel pressure cooker; heat-resistant or stainless-steel mixing bowls; a stainless-steel steamer; a selection of baking tins – loaf tins, baking sheet, bun tray, roasting pan; a wire cooling rack; a selection of storage containers for storing or freezing leftovers.

- Electrically operated equipment – a liquidizer for blending soups and making purées; a food mixer.
- Juicers – raw juices contain many nutritious and health-giving properties, but they can be too concentrated for those prone to food intolerances, so be careful.
- Water filters – some people are affected by the chlorine and fluoride in tap water. A water filter can be helpful to remove these chemicals as well as the residues of fertilizers, pesticides, herbicides, fungicides, industrial waste and radioactive substances that may be present.
- Microwave ovens: there is doubt about the quality of the food when cooked in a microwave oven and so, until more research has been carried out, it is advisable to use other methods of cooking.

Stocking your larder

Good planning can help to pave the way to successfully managing your diet. It is helpful to look ahead and stock your larder with the basic grain cereals, dried beans, lentils, etc. Always have some of your good, 'safe' foods on hand so that if you do start reacting to any particular item, there is something to fall back on. Buy organic produce, including meat, wherever possible, and avoid all processed foods and those containing additives, preservatives and colourings such as margarine. Polyunsaturated oils contain fatty acids which are essential for health, but these can only be found in certain unrefined and cold-pressed oils since the refining process can turn the fatty acids into harmful trans-fatty acids. Oils should be purchased in glass bottles and refrigerated once opened, because any oil or fat can become rancid when exposed to light or air for any length of time. It is also important to use low temperatures when cooking with oil or fat as excessive heat can produce toxins. It is for this reason that the recipes use only low temperatures.

Check sell-buy labels and avoid all sauces and composite foods, eg sausages, burgers, etc. Do also allow your diet to be as varied as possible. The wealth of wholefoods available means that you can eat delicious, exciting meals without having to smother the food in additive-filled sauces. Instead, you will find that you soon begin to appreciate the more subtle and natural flavours of the foods. The following are some of the foods you may want to buy:

Agar-agar is a seaweed-based setting agent similar to gelatine. It is rich in protein and calcium and is easy to digest. It may be bought as granules or flakes. The granules are more processed but stronger. Use one teaspoon of granules to one cup of liquid. With the flakes, use one tablespoon to one cup of liquid. For both types, mix the agar-agar with some or all of the liquid, bring to the boil and simmer for one minute. It sets quickly but may be reheated to liquefy without spoiling.

Amaranth is a relatively new cereal to our stores and is useful for highly sensitive people who are unlikely to have built up an intolerance to it. It is gluten-free, contains all of the eight amino acids and is also rich in iron. It is similar to millet in appearance and can be cooked in the same way. Due to its comparatively high protein content, it is also a useful food for vegans who are intolerant to nuts.

Barley is the major grain used in the manufacture of alcohol. It is a glutinous cereal and can be bought as a flour, flakes, pearl barley or pot barley. As pearl barley has been processed it will not sprout, so it is better to buy pot barley.

Buckwheat is a gluten- and wheat-free seed which can be cooked and treated like rice. It is rich in potassium and the amino acid lysine which most grains lack. It also contains rutin which is good for strengthening the blood capillaries, helps improve circulation and stabilizes blood pressure.

Dairy foods – allergies and intolerances to cows' milk products are extremely common, but the protein in goats' and sheep's milk is more easily digested. Live yoghurt, preferably sheep's or goats', and some cheeses in which the milk has been partially broken down by enzyme action are often tolerated more easily. Both goats' and sheep's milk will freeze, although goats' milk can have a somewhat 'goaty' flavour unless it is very fresh. Clarified butter can often be tolerated by milk-sensitive people. This is because the milk protein has been separated off. It can be bought as 'ghee' at Indian food shops and at most supermarkets or can be made at home by melting a pack of butter over a gentle heat, allowing it to cook slightly and then pouring the liquid carefully into a glass jar. The proteins in the butter will have settled on the bottom of the pan. Ghee and butter are the most stable fats for use in cooking.

Flax seed oil (linseed oil) is one of the richest and most stable sources of omega-3 fatty acids. Use on salads or take by the spoonful, one or two tablespoons a day, but it is not suitable for cooking.

Hemp seed/oil hemp is one of the sturdiest and fastest growing plants on the planet and is well favoured by environmentalists. Its long, penetrating roots draw minerals buried deep in the soil up to the surface, enriching the soil on which it grows and requiring no pesticides, herbicides and little fertilizer. Hemp seeds are rich in magnesium, potassium, sulphur and other key elements and contain all the essential amino acids in an easily digestible form. They contain the richest known source of essential fatty acids in their oil and in the perfect ratio for human nutritional needs. The drug tetrahydracannabinol is contained in the leaves and the flowers of certain strains of the hemp plant and it is for this reason that growing hemp is illegal. However, the drug is not present in the seeds which are legal and obtainable. They are best eaten raw or ground and made into butters. They can be also added to flours to make hemp breads, etc.

Kamut is an ancient, non-hybridized grain, tolerable to many 'wheat-allergic' people. It is now being produced in the United States and slowly coming onto the market in Great Britain. It is a variety of high-protein, low-gluten wheat with kernels two to three times the size of wheat grains. Because of its low gluten content, though, it is not so good for making bread.

Kelp is a natural seaweed product which is extremely high in minerals and trace elements, particularly iodine. It may be used as a substitute for salt.

Millet is gluten-free and cheaper to buy than the other grains mentioned. It can be bought at most food stores. It is the most alkaline of the grains and contains all but one of the essential amino acids. It also contains potassium, iron and magnesium and is an excellent source of silicon, which is a mineral essential for healthy bones, teeth, nails and hair. It can be used in both sweet and savoury dishes. Prepare as for rice, using one cup of millet to two cups of water, and cook for 25 minutes.

Miso is a Japanese seasoning paste, similar to yeast extract in taste and colour. It is made from fermented rice, barley or soya beans, so check the label carefully when buying. It is an excellent source of nutrients and is useful as a flavouring for soups and stews.

Olive oil is rich in monounsaturates, though low in essential fatty acids. The cold-pressed, virgin olive oil is the only unrefined oil sold on the mass market. Due to its relative stability and to the ease with which it can be extracted, ie it does not require high-pressure equipment, many of its health-giving properties remain intact. It contains vitamin E, phytosterols, chlorophyll, magnesium, carotene and other beneficial minor ingredients unique to olives. Use virgin olive oil on salads, for stirring into vegetables and soups and for low-temperature cooking as well.

Pepper – black and white pepper can be used on cold or warm food. However, it is important not to heat it or add it to very hot food as it then becomes an irritant to the intestinal mucosa.

Pulses (dried peas, beans and lentils) are a good source of protein and fibre. When mixed with a grain such as rice, they provide a complete protein meal, ie one that contains all the essential amino acids. It is recommended that these are sprouted for two or three days prior to cooking or for three to five days for eating raw.

Quinoa can be used in the same way as millet. It contains all eight essential amino acids and is extremely rich in calcium and iron. It can be cooked in the granule form or the seeds can be ground to a flour in a liquidizer or coffee grinder.

Rice is one of the oldest cultivated grains. Generally speaking, it is a safe food for most people, but those who have used it as a staple food for many years may need to check carefully for any intolerance. Choose organically grown, short- or long-grain varieties. Wholegrain, basmati and wild rice and wholegrain noodles are also available in healthfood stores. Vermicelli (white Chinese noodles) may be useful in some recipes. Always wash rice grains before cooking. Soaking for six to eight hours prior to cooking will bring the rice 'alive' and reduce cooking time. To cook rice, use one cup of rice to two and a quarter cups of water and a pinch of salt. Place the rice in a heavy-based pan. Add the water and bring to the boil. Cover and simmer gently for about 30 minutes until all the water has been absorbed. Use a wooden spoon or spatula to remove the rice from the pan.

Safflower, soya bean and sunflower seed oils are highly nutritious and rich in polyunsaturates and essential fatty acids, but only when unrefined and cold-pressed. Use in salads and add to soups and vegetables when off the boil. If you do need to use these oils in baking keep the temperature of the oven below 160° C (325°F), Gas Mark 3.

Sesame oil should be unrefined, untoasted and cold-pressed. In this state it is a rich source of omega-6 essential fatty acids. Use cold, sprinkled on salads. It remains reasonably stable when heated so it can be used for low-temperature cooking.

Sorghum is an African grain, now grown in many other parts of the world. It is similar in composition to corn but higher in protein and is available at some healthfood stores or by mail order.

Spelt wheat is an ancient precursor of modern-day wheat. It is usually grown organically and is often more easily tolerated than ordinary wheat.

Sweet potatoes, yams, eddoes and dasheen are available in most large supermarkets and are sold at many West Indian food stores. They are all high in carbohydrates and may be used like potatoes. It is also possible to buy sweet potato and yam flours. The flesh of the sweet potato is either whitish or orange, and due to its sweet flavour it may be used in sweet or savoury cooking.

Tahini is a nut butter made from ground roasted sesame seeds and oil, and may be used as a spread, as a topping, in dips and dressings, and in sauces and soups.

Tamari is a naturally produced, wheat-free soya sauce.

Tempeh is cultured from cooked, split soya beans in a similar way to cheese.

Tofu is a high-protein, low-fat curd made from soya milk. Both tofu and tempeh are very digestible.

Tropical oils – unrefined and cold-pressed palm oil or coconut oil are much more stable when heated than any of the polyunsaturated oils and are therefore more suitable for cooking purposes. If you are able to obtain these, you can use them in the baking recipes instead of sunflower and safflower oils.

Umeboshi plums are Japanese plums which have been picked green and pickled in brine with shiso (perilla) leaves which give them their pink colour. They are rich in enzymes and are a good digestive aid. They may be bought at healthfood shops, either whole or as a purée.

Walnut oil is an excellent source of omega-6 and a smaller amount of omega-3 essential fatty acids as long as it is unrefined and cold-pressed.

Wheat contains gluten, but when the grains are sprouted the gluten and gluten-like substances, also found in rye, barley and oats, are broken down by the enzyme action. You may therefore find that you can tolerate wheat grains and similarly rye, barley and oats, when they are sprouted. In addition, some people find that they can tolerate durum wheat found in wheat pasta, couscous, bulgur wheat and semolina more easily than the strong wheat flour used in baking. Bread made with French flour may also be an alternative. Wheat seems to absorb more of the pesticides and artificial fertilizers used in farming than other grains, so it is important to buy organically grown wheat.

Wheatgerm oil is one of the richest sources of vitamin E and may also protect the heart and help nerve regeneration. Many people who are intolerant to the wheat grain find that they can tolerate wheatgerm oil. Take by the spoonful or cold on salads.

General guidelines

Rinse all grains and seeds before use and wash fruit and vegetables thoroughly: 1 tbsp vinegar or 500mg of vitamin C powder to 1 litre of water can be used to help remove heavy metals and pesticide residues. The best way to cook vegetables is to steam or boil them in a little water and any leftover water can then be used as stock.

Frying demands the use of high temperatures, so it is best to avoid it if you can. If you do need to fry, you can cool-fry by putting a little water into the pan with the fat or oil. This applies to cooking in a wok as well. Butter or ghee, pure lard, tropical fats (coconut, palm kernel), sesame and olive oil, in that order, are the best oils to use as they produce the least amount of toxic substances when heated. However, take care not to use too much of the saturated fats (butter, lard and tropical fats) as they can have a congesting effect on your body.

Your stock pot

You may want to make up your own stock to use in soups and other recipes. These can then be conveniently frozen and used when needed. Label with care, listing all the ingredients and the day when the stock can be used.

Meat stock

Use raw bones from organically reared mutton, lamb, beef or pork (according to the day), chopped into 5cm (2in) pieces. Wash and place in a large heavy saucepan or pressure cooker. Cover with cold water and a pinch of salt and bring to the boil. Simmer for three hours or for 1½ hours in a pressure cooker. Strain the stock and allow to cool. Skim off the fat before use.

Poultry or game stock

Rabbit, hare, turkey, duck, goose, chicken or game stock can
be made from the carcass and giblets, and from the skin and
legs of poultry and game birds. Cook for 1½ hours (45 minutes
in a pressure cooker), strain, allow to cool and skim off the
fat.

Fish stock

Wash the trimmings and break up the bones. Cover with cold
water, add a little sea salt and bring to simmering point. Cook
gently for 20 to 30 minutes. Overcooking can cause bitterness.

Vegetable stock

Use the leftover cooking water from any vegetables, vegetable
trimmings, seaweeds, pasta and grains listed for the day.
Simmer gently with plenty of water and with the lid on the
saucepan for one and a half to two hours. The nutrients will
leach into the stock which can then be strained off and the
fibre remains discarded.

Soaking and sprouting beans, grains and seeds

Many beans, grains, seeds and even some nuts will sprout.
This process greatly enhances and increases the nutrient value
and digestibility of these foods.

The water used activates the germination process, and
many of the enzyme and metabolic inhibitors are washed out,
including phytates and oxalates. These are designed to keep
the seed from germinating until the allotted time. When
ingested, they may block our absorption of calcium, zinc and
other minerals. After the initial germination, other enzymes
come into force which start the predigestion of the proteins,
fats and carbohydrates into amino acids, fatty acids and
simple carbohydrates respectively. The synthesis of many
vitamins takes place, including vitamin B complex, and
vitamins C and E. Together with the mineral content, which
may be hardly measurable in the dormant seed, these increase
remarkably, reaching a peak around the fourth and fifth day

of sprouting. Yes, even though the seeds and beans may only have been given distilled water!

Alfalfa, linseeds, fenugreek, sesame, pumpkin, sunflower and oats will need at least six hours soaking time. Beans, almonds and other nuts, wheat, rice, millet and rye will need at least 12 hours. Special bean sprouters may be purchased for this purpose but simply using a jam jar can be just as effective. Take a handful of beans, wash them thoroughly and place them in a jam jar. Cover the beans with about three times as much water. Place a piece of muslin or screen over the top for draining and fix it in place with an elastic band. Leave the beans to soak overnight. Rinse and drain the beans through the muslin top and place the jar on its side in a dark, airy cupboard. Repeat this twice a day for three to five days. For the last two days, place the jar in sunlight, making sure to keep the beans moist while they grow green with chlorophyll. Refrigerate the beans in a covered container and use them raw in salads, soups, etc.

It is advantageous to sprout all beans for two or three days prior to cooking. Many people who may have difficulty digesting beans will find them acceptable when prepared in this way.

The 4-Day Rotation Diet Plan

	DAY 1	DAY 2	DAY 3	DAY 4
Cereals, grains and flour	Millet Wheat, spelt wheat Barley Rye Kamut	Corn (maize) Oats Green banana flour Quinoa Sorghum Arrowroot	Rice Wild rice Sago flour Any pulse flour	Amaranth Buckwheat Tapioca Chestnut flour
Meat	Rabbit/hare Crustacean family Mollusc family Freshwater fish Yeast	Pork, wild boar Venison	Bird family Eggs	Beef, veal Lamb Saltwater fish Dairy products
Nuts and seeds	Cashew family Sesame	Brazil nuts Pine nuts Macadamia nuts Tiger nuts Pumpkin seeds Hemp seed	Almond Coconut Sunflower	Hazelnut Chestnut Walnut family Poppy seeds
Sugars	Malt barley Cane sugar	Fruit sugar Corn syrup Oat syrup	Honey Date syrup Beet sugar Rice syrup	Maple syrup Apple/pear concentrate

Drinks	Tea Green leaf tea	Oat milk Hibiscus tea Mint teas Lemon verbena	Soya milk Rice milk Rooibosch tea Cocoa	Sheep's milk Goats' milk Coffee Equisetum tea
Vegetables	Parsley family Seaweed, kelp Mushrooms	Mallow family Melon family Potato family Lily family Laurel family Olives	Aster family Beet family Pea family	Arum family Mustard family Sweet potato Yam Sorrel
Herbs and spices	Parsley family Pepper family	Mint family Ginger family Juniper berries	Tarragon Fenugreek Nutmeg family	Lemon grass Myrtle family Capers
Fruit	Citrus family Blueberry family Mulberry family Elderberry Pomegranate Passion fruit Papaya Mango	Gooseberry family Banana family Pineapple Cape gooseberries Kiwi fruit	Plum family Dates Grape family	Apple family Rose family Guava Lychees Rhubarb
Oils, etc (should be cold-pressed and glass-bottled)	Sesame oil Wheatgerm oil	Olive oil Hemp-seed oil Flax-seed (linseed) oil	Sunflower oil Safflower oil Soya oil Almond oil Tropical oils Wine vinegar Balsamic vinegar	Walnut oil Hazelnut oil Cider vinegar Raspberry vinegar

CHAPTER 3

Recipes for the 4-Day Plan

Day 1

The following foods can be eaten:

Cereals, grains and flour Wheat; semolina and couscous; bulgur wheat; spelt wheat flour; kamut; barley; rye; Ryevita; pumpernickel bread; millet; wheat, rye, barley, millet and kamut pasta.

Meat, fish Rabbit and hare; the crustacean family (crab, crayfish, lobster, prawn, shrimp); the mollusc family abalone, snail, squid, clam, mussel, oyster, octopus, scallop); freshwater fish (salmon, trout, pike, perch, bass).

Nuts and seeds Cashew nuts; pistachio nuts; sesame seeds and spread (tahini).

Sugars Barley malt; cane sugar.

Drinks Barleycup; tea; green leaf tea; fennel tea; lime tea; orange juice.

Vegetables The parsley family (carrots, parsnips, celery, celeriac, fennel); seaweed, kelp; mushrooms.

Herbs and spices Aniseed; caraway; dill; cumin; coriander; chervil; fennel leaf or seed.

Fruit The citrus family (lemon, orange, grapefruit, lime, tangerine, citron); mango; papaya; star fruit; passion fruit; pomegranate; fig; breadfruit; mulberry; cranberry; blueberry; elderberry.

Oils Sesame oil, wheatgerm oil.

Breakfasts

Grapefruit and orange fruit salad
Frumenty
Millet and kamut porridge
Barley flake muesli
Grilled mushrooms on toast
Grilled trout

Soups and starters

Mushroom and barley broth
Parsnip and coriander soup
Clear vegetable and nori broth
Carrot and orange soup
Cream of celeriac and lovage soup
Fish and fennel soup
Pistachio and rabbit paté
Mini crab cakes
Papaya and grapefruit salad
Stuffed mushrooms
Spiced scallops

Main meals

Pot-roast rabbit with mushroom and fennel stuffing
Rabbit/hare hotpot
Grilled trout fillets with tropical fruit
Poached salmon with dill sauce
Stuffed squid

Vegetarian main meals

Millet croquettes
Barley, cashew and vegetable loaf
Mushroom fricassee with bulgur wheat
Cashew nut and celery flan
Mixed vegetable terrine

Vegetables and salads

Salad dressing
Carrot, celery and coriander salad
Orange and fennel salad
Braised celery
Mixed grain salad
Seafood salad

Puddings and desserts

Fig and lime sorbet
Orange fruit jelly
Blood oranges with cranberries
Pistachio nut semolina with lime
Blueberry pie

Breads, cakes and biscuits

Pitta bread
Soda bread
Sprouted grain bread
Barley and cashew nut scones
Rye bread
Carrot and fig slice
Orange and cashew nut crunchies

Drinks and miscellaneous

Cashew nut milk
Cashew nut cream
Carrot and cashew nut spread
Mushroom and tahini spread
Lemon and orange barley water
Lemon and elderflower cordial
Elderberry punch

Breakfasts

Grapefruit and orange fruit salad

4 oranges
2–3 grapefruit
juice of 2 oranges

Segment the fruit by cutting away both ends to the flesh.
Working from top to bottom, cut away the peel and the pith
following the curve of the fruit. Working over a bowl to catch
the juice, hold the fruit in your hand and cut down each side
of the segments, cutting them away from the membrane and
discarding the membrane and any seeds.

Arrange the segments in a serving bowl and pour over the
orange juice.

Frumenty

225g (8oz; 1 cup) organic whole wheat grains
1 litre (1¾ pints; 4 cups) water

Wash the wheat grains and pre-soak for 6 to 8 hours. Place
them in a pan with the remaining water and bring to the boil.
Simmer gently for 10 minutes and then leave in a warm place
overnight.

At the end of this time, the wheat grains should have burst
open and look starchy and white, and formed a thick jelly. If
some are still whole, boil them up again and cook gently for a
little while longer.

Frumenty may be eaten for breakfast or supper, served with
fruit.

Millet and kamut porridge

(serves 2)
75g (3oz; ¾ cup) millet flakes
25g (1oz; ⅛ cup) kamut, soaked overnight
500ml (1 pint; 2 cups) water

Place the millet and kamut in a saucepan and add the water.
Bring to the boil and simmer for 4 or 5 minutes until the
kamut is soft and the porridge thickens.

Serve with barley malt, chopped figs or cashew nut milk.

Barley flake muesli

2 cups barley flakes or a mixture of flakes from wheat, rye or
millet grains; cashew nuts; ground linseeds; sesame seeds;
chopped, dried or fresh figs and mango

Mix together and serve with mango or orange juice, or cashew
nut milk.

Grilled mushrooms on toast

225g (8oz; 4 cups) wild mushrooms, brushed clean
1 tbsp sesame seed oil
1 tbsp water
2 tbsp fresh parsley, chopped
4 slices spelt wheat toast

Warm the oil and water in a pan and gently cook the mushrooms for a couple of minutes. Add the chopped parsley and serve on pieces of toast.

Grilled trout

4 medium-sized freshwater trout
1 tbsp fresh dill, chopped, or 1 tsp dried
1 tbsp sesame seeds
sea salt or kelp

Place the trout in a grill pan. Make two or three slashes across the skin and sprinkle with salt. Grill on one side only for 5 to 7 minutes until just cooked through. There should be no need to turn the trout. Sprinkle with dill and sesame seeds and serve.

Soups and starters

Mushroom and barley broth

225g (8oz; 4 cups) mushrooms, diced
175g (6oz; ¾ cup) pot barley
2 carrots, diced
1 litre (1¾ pints; 4 cups) stock or water
2 tbsp chopped parsley
sea salt or 1 tsp barley miso

Put all the ingredients into a casserole dish, cover with a lid and bring to the boil. Simmer gently for 40 to 50 minutes until the barley is cooked, adding more liquid if necessary. Serve with a sprinkling of chopped parsley.

Parsnip and coriander soup

675g (1½lb; 6 cups) parsnips, diced
2 sticks celery, sliced
1 litre (1¾ pints; 4 cups) vegetable stock
½ tsp ground coriander
½ tsp ground cumin
2 tbsp fresh coriander leaves, chopped
sea salt or kelp

Place half the stock in a pan and bring to the boil. Add the parsnips, celery, salt and ground spices and cook until tender. Cool slightly and then liquidize to a purée. Return to the pan with the remaining stock and reheat. Serve with a garnishing of fresh coriander.

Clear vegetable and nori broth

2 large carrots, cut into matchsticks
2 sticks celery, thinly sliced
1 small parsnip, diced
2–3 sheets nori seaweed, cut into 2.5 cm (1in) squares
1 litre (1¾ pints; 4 cups) vegetable, lamb or fish stock or water
1 tbsp sesame oil
sea salt, kelp or 1 tsp barley miso

Place some of the water/stock in a pan and bring to the boil. Add the vegetables and cook until tender. Add the remaining stock and the sea salt, kelp or barley miso and nori seaweed, bring to the boil and simmer for 1 minute. Stir in the sesame seed oil and serve.

Carrot and orange soup

450g (1lb; 4 cups) carrots, diced
2 sticks celery, sliced
juice of 3 oranges
grated rind of 1 orange

1 litre (1¾ pints; 4 cups) vegetable stock
1 tbsp sesame oil
sea salt

Bring the stock to the boil and add the carrot and celery and cook until tender. Cool slightly and liquidize to a purée. Return to the pan to reheat and then stir in the orange juice, sesame oil and salt. Serve with a sprinkling of grated orange rind.

Cream of celeriac and lovage soup

450g (1lb; 4 cups) celeriac, peeled and diced
2 sticks celery, sliced
1 litre (1¾ pints; 4 cups) stock or water
2 tbsp fresh lovage, chopped
sea salt

Bring some of the water to the boil and add the vegetables. Simmer until soft, cool slightly and then liquidize until smooth. Return to the saucepan and add the remaining liquid, lovage and salt. Bring to the boil and cook for 3 or 4 minutes. Serve garnished with a sprinkling of lovage.

Fish and fennel soup

125g (4oz) freshwater fish, filleted
125g (4oz; 1 cup) mixed shellfish, shelled
1 litre (1¾ pints; 4 cups) fish or vegetable stock or water
1 head of fennel, cut into strips
2 carrots, diced
50g (2oz; 1 cup) small pasta shells
2 tbsp fresh parsley, chopped
1 tsp dried fennel
sea salt or 1 tsp kelp

Bring some of the water to the boil and cook the vegetables until just tender. Add the remaining liquid, dried fennel and salt and re-boil. Add the fish and pasta, and cook for another 5 minutes, adding the parsley during the last minute of cooking. Cook the pasta separately if a larger, longer-cooking variety is used instead of the small shells.

Pistachio and rabbit paté

450g (1lb) boneless rabbit meat and/or rabbit liver, diced
75g (3oz; ¾ cup) pistachio nuts, chopped
125g (4oz; 1 cup) celeriac, diced
1 tbsp sesame oil
250ml (½ pint) water or stock
1 rounded tbsp barley or wheat flour
2 tbsp chopped parsley
sea salt
black pepper

Warm the oil and a little water in a pan and gently cook the
rabbit meat on both sides for 4 or 5 minutes. Put to one side
and cook the celeriac in the juices until soft. Add the stock
and parsley and bring to the boil. Simmer for 2 or 3 minutes.
Mix the flour with a little cold water and stir into the liquid to
make a thick sauce. Cool slightly and liquidize with the meat
to make a smooth paste. Turn into a bowl and stir in the
pistachio nuts, salt and pepper. Serve chilled with bread or
crackers.

Mini crab cakes

225g (8oz; 1½ cups) cooked crab meat
75g (3oz; ¾ cup) fresh breadcrumbs
1 tbsp flour
grated zest and juice of 1 lime
½ tsp ground cumin
½ tsp ground coriander
sea salt or kelp
lime slices and coriander leaves for garnishing

Preheat the oven to 160° C (325° F), Gas Mark 3.
   Mix the ingredients together and form the mixture into
eight small, flat fishcakes. Bake in the oven for 20 minutes.
Serve with slices of lime and sprigs of coriander.

Papaya and grapefruit salad

3 pink grapefruit
2 papayas

the juice of 1 lime
julienne strips of lime zest
1 tbsp sesame oil
1 tsp peppercorns, crushed
sea salt
sprigs of fennel or dill for garnishing

Peel the rind from the grapefruit and divide the flesh into segments. Peel the papayas, scoop out the seeds and cut the flesh into thin slices. Arrange on serving plates with the grapefruit. Mix the juices, peppercorns, salt and sesame oil together and pour over the fruit. Garnish with sprigs of fennel or dill and the strips of lime zest.

Stuffed mushrooms

8 large flat mushrooms
1 cup cooked millet
2 tbsp fresh coriander, chopped
1 tbsp sesame seeds
1 tbsp tahini
sea salt
lemon wedges

Preheat the oven to 160° C (325° F), Gas Mark 3.

Peel the mushrooms and remove the stalks. Chop the stalks and steam or boil them in a little water until soft. Place in a bowl and mix with the millet, tahini, coriander and salt. Place the mixture on the gills of the mushrooms and sprinkle with sesame seeds. Bake for 20 minutes until the mushrooms are cooked and the stuffing is crisp. Serve with lemon wedges.

Spiced scallops

8 scallops, shelled and cleaned
1 level tbsp plain unbleached white flour or barley flour
1 tsp cane sugar (optional)
juice and zest of 1 lemon
½ tsp ground cumin
½ tsp ground coriander
2 tsp chopped dill
sea salt

TO GARNISH:
sprigs of dill
lemon wedges

Poach the scallops in half a cup of water for 1 minute.

Mix the cumin, coriander, sugar and flour with a little cold water. Add the water from the scallops and cook, stirring until the sauce thickens. Stir in the scallops, lemon zest, salt and juice and the chopped dill. Cook until the mixture comes to the boil.

Divide into individual dishes and garnish with wedges of lemon and sprigs of dill.

Scallops are in season from November to March but can be bought frozen throughout the year.

Main meals

Pot-roast rabbit with mushroom and fennel stuffing

1 large rabbit, skinned and cleaned
500ml (1 pint; 2 cups) stock or water
FOR THE STUFFING:
125g (4oz; 1 cup) breadcrumbs or millet flakes
125g (4oz; 2 cups) mushrooms, chopped
zest and juice of 1 lemon
1 bulb fennel, chopped
3 tbsp fresh parsley chopped
1 tsp chopped chervil (if available)
sea salt

Preheat the oven to 180°C (350°F), Gas Mark 4.

Mix together the ingredients for the stuffing, adding a little water to bind it if necessary. Stuff the body of the rabbit and bring the open sides together, securing with string or skewers. Place in a casserole dish, pour over the stock and cover. Cook in the oven for 15 minutes. Reduce the temperature to 160°C (325°F), Gas Mark 3, and cook for a further 45 minutes. Allow the rabbit to rest for 10 minutes before carving.

Rabbit/hare hotpot

900g (2lb) rabbit/hare portions
1 litre (1¾ pints; 4 cups) boiling water
1 parsnip, diced
4 carrots, sliced
3 sticks celery, sliced
125g (4oz; ½ cup) pot barley
2 tbsp freshly chopped parsley
sea salt or kelp

Arrange the rabbit or hare portions in a heavy-based saucepan. Add the vegetables, barley and salt and pour over the boiling water. Bring to the boil and simmer gently for 1½ hours. Add the chopped parsley and serve.

Grilled trout fillets with tropical fruit

4 fillets of wild trout
1 large mango
1 star fruit, sliced
1 tsp ground coriander
2 tbsp fresh coriander leaves, chopped
sea salt

To prepare the mango, hold the fruit upright and take a slice off each side, cutting as near to the stone as possible, then cut the smaller pieces off the ends. Remove the skin and cut the flesh into matchstick pieces. Arrange the pieces, together with the star fruit, on a serving dish.

Place the trout in a grill pan, sprinkle with salt and ground coriander. Grill for 5 to 7 minutes.
Arrange the pieces of fish over the fruit and garnish with chopped coriander leaves.

Poached salmon with dill sauce

4 wild salmon steaks
1 tbsp lemon juice
sea salt
FOR THE SAUCE:
50g (2oz; ½ cup) wheat or barley flour
500ml (1 pint; 2 cups) cashew nut milk, fish or vegetable stock
2 tbsp freshly chopped dill
sea salt

Place the salmon steaks in a large saucepan and pour on
sufficient water to cover. Add the salt and lemon juice and
poach for 5 to 10 minutes until just cooked through. Strain off
the water to use in the sauce. Keep the salmon warm on a
serving dish.

For the sauce, mix the flour with a little of the stock and
stir into the poaching water. Gradually stir in the rest of the
stock, return to moderate heat and stir briskly until the sauce
thickens. Add the dill and the salt and pour the sauce over the
salmon and serve.

Stuffed squid

1kg (2.2lb) small squid, cleaned and prepared
3 carrots, cut into matchsticks
250ml (½ pint; 1 cup) vegetable stock
chopped parsley for garnishing
lemon wedges
FOR THE STUFFING:
50g (2oz; ½ cup) breadcrumbs or cooked millet
2 sticks celery, finely diced
2 tbsp fresh parsley, chopped
3 tbsp sesame oil
rind of 1 lemon
sea salt or kelp

Preheat the oven to 160°C (325°F), Gas Mark 3.

Mix together the ingredients for the stuffing and stuff the
squid bodies with the mixture. Sew up or fasten the openings
with a cocktail stick. Place in an ovenproof dish with the
carrots and pour over the stock. Bake for 45 minutes and
serve hot with a sprinkling of parsley and lemon wedges.

Vegetarian main meals

Millet croquettes

225g (8oz; 1 cup) millet, cooked
3 sticks celery, diced
3 carrots, grated
2 tbsp millet flour
1–2 tbsp tahini
1 tbsp fresh parsley chopped
125ml (¼ pint; ½ cup) water
sea salt or kelp
25g (1oz; ¼ cup) sesame seeds for coating

Preheat the oven to 150°C (300°F), Gas Mark 2.
Mix all the ingredients together and form into croquettes. Roll them in the sesame seeds and bake for 25 minutes.

Barley, cashew and vegetable loaf

225g (8oz; 1 cup) pot barley, cooked
125g (4oz; 2 cups) shiitake mushrooms, diced
125g (4oz; 1 cup) cashew nuts, chopped
2 carrots, grated
2 tbsp barley flour
2 tbsp freshly chopped coriander leaves
125ml (¼ pint; ½ cup) stock or water
sea salt or 1 tsp barley miso

Preheat the oven to 160°C (325°F), Gas Mark 3.

Mix all the ingredients together and turn the mixture into a lined 2lb loaf tin. Bake for about 50 minutes until firm.

Mushroom fricassee with bulgur wheat

225g (8oz; 1 cup) bulgur wheat
500ml (1 pint; 2 cups) boiling water
grated rind and juice of 1 lemon
sea salt
275g (10oz; 5 cups) mushrooms, sliced
1 tbsp sesame oil
1 tbsp water
2 tsp barley or wheat flour
125ml (¼ pint; ½ cup) cashew nut milk or stock
1 tbsp freshly chopped parsley

Put the bulgur wheat in a large bowl and pour over the boiling water. Add the lemon rind and a pinch of salt and leave for 15 minutes until all the water has been absorbed.

Cook the mushrooms in a little oil and water until soft. Stir in the flour and nut milk or stock and bring to the boil. Cook for 1 or 2 minutes. Stir in the lemon juice and serve with the bulgur wheat and a garnishing of parsley and lemon wedges.

Couscous (wheat) or millet may be used instead of bulgur wheat.

Cashew nut and celery flan

FOR THE PASTRY:
225g (8oz; 2 cups) wheat or barley flour
4 tbsp sesame oil
water to mix
pinch of salt
FOR THE FILLING:
4 sticks celery, diced and cooked
125g (4oz; 1 cup) cashew nuts
2 tbsp parsley, freshly chopped

FOR THE SAUCE:
50g (2oz; ½ cup) wheat or barley flour
500ml (1 pint) cashew nut milk or vegetable stock
sea salt

Preheat the oven to 160° C (325° F), Gas Mark 3.

For the pastry, rub the oil into the flour and salt and form into a firm dough with a little water. Roll out the pastry and line a 20cm (8in) flan dish. Bake blind (by covering the pastry with greaseproof paper and weighting it with baking beans) and cooking in the oven for 25 minutes.

For the sauce, heat the cashew nut milk/stock in a pan. Mix the flour and salt with a little cold water and stir into the milk. Stir briskly until the sauce thickens.

Spread the celery and cashew nuts evenly over the pastry base and sprinkle with parsley. Cover with the sauce and bake for a further 25 minutes.

Mixed vegetable terrine

350g (12oz; 3 cups) carrots, chopped
350g (12oz; 3 cups) parsnips, chopped
350g (12oz; 3 cups) celeriac, chopped
3 tsp barley or wheat flour
2 sheets nori seaweed
3 tbsp sesame oil
2 tbsp freshly chopped parsley
sea salt

Preheat the oven to 160°C (325°F), Gas Mark 3.

Steam the vegetables in separate pans, drain and allow to cool. Blend each one separately in a blender, adding 1 tsp of flour, 1 tbsp of oil and a pinch of salt to each. Blend the parsley with the celeriac.

Line the base of a 1.4kg (3lb) loaf tin. Carefully spoon in the purées starting with a parsnip layer, then the carrot and finally the celeriac, placing a sheet of nori seaweed between each layer. Bake for 1½ hours until firm.

Allow to cool and then refrigerate. Turn out of the tin when thoroughly cold.

Vegetables and salads

Salad dressing

juice of 2 lemons
4 tbsp oil (wheatgerm oil and/or sesame oil)
1 tbsp tahini (optional)
½ tsp sea salt
black pepper

Combine all the ingredients in a jar and shake well. Use where indicated in the following recipes.

Carrot, celery and coriander salad

225g (8oz; 2 cups) carrots
2 sticks celery
2 tbsp fresh coriander, chopped
salad dressing

Make flower-shaped carrot slices by cutting several grooves lengthways along each carrot, then using a grater to slice them into thin slices. Cut the celery into matchsticks and arrange on a serving dish with the carrot and coriander. Pour over the dressing.

Orange and fennel salad

4 heads of fennel, sliced
2 large oranges, peeled and divided into segments
1 tbsp sprouted fennel seeds (optional)
2–3 sprigs of fennel leaf for garnishing
salad dressing

Arrange the fennel and oranges on a plate, top with sprouted fennel seeds and garnish with the sprigs of fennel leaf. Pour over the salad dressing and serve.

Braised celery

4 celery hearts, trimmed
250ml (½ pint) stock or water
2 tbsp sesame oil
25g (1oz; ¼ cup) wheat, barley, millet or rye flour
sea salt

Preheat the oven to 160°C (325°F), Gas Mark 3.
 Place the celery in a well-oiled casserole dish. Warm the oil in a pan, stir in the flour and cook for a few minutes. Then gradually stir in the stock and salt and cook until the sauce thickens. Pour over the celery and bake in the oven for 1 hour.

Mixed grain salad

125g (4oz; ¾ cup) wheat, barley or rye grains, cooked
125g (4oz; ¾ cup) cooked millet
50g (2oz; ½ cup) cashew nuts, roughly chopped
1–2 tbsp sprouted seeds (dill, celery, aniseed)
2 sticks celery, diced
50g (2oz; ½ cup) grated carrot
freshly chopped parsley
1 tbsp sesame seeds
salad dressing

Mix all the ingredients together, keeping the sesame seeds and parsley for garnishing. Pour over the salad dressing. The grains may also be used, sprouted.

Seafood salad

225g (8oz; 4 cups) pasta spirals – wheat, rye, barley or millet
sea salt
450g (1lb) mussels
8–10 baby squid tentacles, cut from the bodies
225g (8oz; 2 cups) peeled prawns
2 tbsp freshly chopped parsley
salad dressing

To cook the pasta, fill a large pan with water and bring to the boil. Add the pasta and a pinch of salt. Cook until just tender (*al dente*), for 8 to 10 minutes according to the type of pasta used. Allow to cool.

To prepare the mussels, pull off the beards and thoroughly wash and scrub the shells. Discard any shells that are open. Place in a shallow pan and cover with boiling water. Cook for five minutes, shaking the pan now and then. Remove the mussels as soon as the shells open and discard any that have remained shut.

Place the squid in the water used for cooking the mussels and cook for 15 minutes until tender. Add the prawns and cook for a further 5 minutes. Drain and allow to cool. Cut the squid into rings and mix with the mussels, prawns and cooked pasta.

Arrange the salad on a serving dish. Pour over the salad dressing and sprinkle with chopped parsley.

Puddings and desserts

Fig and lime sorbet

6 fresh figs
2 limes
cane sugar to taste
2 level tsp agar-agar
FOR DECORATION:
1 fresh fig
julienne strips of lime

Wash and cut the figs into quarters and place them in a saucepan and cover with water. Cover, bring to the boil and cook gently for 5 minutes.

Allow the figs and liquid to cool a little, then liquidize, adding the lime juice, sugar and agar-agar dissolved in a little hot water. Spoon the mixture into a freezer container and freeze for 1 to 2 hours until almost frozen. Return to the liquidizer and whip until light and fluffy. Return to the freezer until firm.

Serve the sorbet in scoops and decorate with thin slices of fig and julienne strips of lime.

Orange fruit jelly

3 medium-size sweet oranges
zest of ½ an orange
250ml (½ pint; 1 cup) orange juice
3 tsp granulated agar-agar or 3 tbsp flaked agar-agar
125ml (¼ pint; 1 cup) water

Peel the oranges and cut the flesh into half segments. Place in a serving bowl with the orange juice.

Take the zest and cut into fine julienne strips. Place in a small saucepan with the agar-agar and the water. Bring to the boil and simmer for 2 minutes. Cool slightly and then quickly stir into the oranges and juice. Leave to set in a cool place for 6 hours.

Blood oranges with cranberries

4 blood oranges
zest of 1 orange
175g (6oz; 1½ cups) cranberries
1 tbsp raw cane sugar

Peel the oranges and cut the flesh into segments. Cut the zest into julienne strips. Cook the cranberries in a little water for 2 or 3 minutes with the zest and the sugar. Allow to cool and then mix with the oranges.

On Day 2 of the diet, a little cinnamon may be added.

Pistachio nut semolina with lime

2 tbsp semolina
500ml (1 pint; 2 cups) cashew nut milk
125g (4oz; 1 cup) unsalted pistachio nuts, chopped
zest of 1 lime, cut into julienne strips juice of 2 limes
2 tbsp raw cane sugar

Bring the cashew nut milk to the boil and add the zest of lime. Add the sugar and sprinkle in the semolina, stirring briskly until the mixture thickens. Allow the semolina to cool, then stir in the lime juice and chopped pistachio nuts, keeping back a few for decoration.

Blueberry pie

225g (8oz; 2 cups) blueberries
50g (2oz; ½ cup) ground cashew nuts
1 tbsp raw cane sugar
grated zest and juice of 1 lemon
250ml (½ pint; 1 cup) water
1 tsp agar-agar granules
1 cooked pastry case (see recipe for celery and cashew nut flan
    on page 42)

Line the bottom of the pastry case with the ground cashew nuts.

Place the blueberries in a pan with the water, agar-agar, sugar and lemon zest and bring to the boil. Simmer for a couple of minutes until the blueberries are soft. Cool slightly, stir in the lemon juice and pour into the flan case. Allow to set and serve with cashew nut cream (*see* page 49).

Breads, cakes and biscuits

Pitta bread

450g (1lb; 4 cups) organic strong wholewheat flour or
    barley flour
25g (1oz) fresh or dried yeast
250ml (½ pint; 1 cup) warm water
1 tsp unrefined molasses sugar
1 tsp salt

HERB AND SESAME TOPPING (optional):
2 tsp sesame oil
2 tbsp sesame seeds
2 tbsp chopped fresh parsley or coriander leaves

Preheat the oven to 220°C (425°F), Gas Mark 7.

Mix the yeast, sugar and water and leave in a warm place for 5 to 10 minutes until frothy.

Mix the salt with the flour and combine with the yeast liquid to form a soft dough. Knead for 10 minutes, then place in a large oiled polythene bag and leave in a warm place until doubled in size.

On a floured board, knead the dough for a minute and divide it into eight portions. Knead each portion into a small ball and roll out into an oval shape. Lay these onto several oiled baking trays. Cover with oiled polythene and leave to rest for 30 minutes.

Brush with sesame oil and sprinkle with herbs and sesame seeds. Bake for 8 minutes until risen and puffed.

Soda bread

450g (1lb; 4 cups) wheat, barley, rye or millet flour
1 tsp bicarbonate of soda
½ tsp salt
250ml (½ pint; 1 cup) water or nut milk

Preheat the oven to 170°C (340°F), Gas Mark 3.

Mix all the ingredients together and kneed into a firm dough. Shape into a flat round loaf, cut a deep cross on top and bake for 40 minutes until firm.

Sprouted grain bread

450g (1lb; 2 cups) organic wheat grains
225g (8oz; 1 cup) rye grains
225g (8oz; 1 cup) barley grains
filtered water for sprouting
sea salt

Rinse the grains and leave to soak for 15 hours. Drain off the water and leave to sprout for two or three days, rinsing morning and evening, until the grains have developed 2.5cm (1in) sprouts.

Preheat the oven to 130°C (260°F), Gas Mark 1.

Place the sprouts in a meat mincer and grind to a fine texture. Add the salt and place in one large or two small well-oiled loaf tins and bake for 4 or 5 hours until the bread leaves the sides of the tin. The loaf could also be cooked overnight on the lower shelf of an Aga.

Cashew nuts, figs, linseeds or sesame seeds may be added to the recipe.

Barley and cashew nut scones

225g (8oz; 2 cups) barley flour
1 tsp bicarbonate of soda
125g (4oz; 1 cup) cashew nuts, ground or chopped
4 tbsp sesame oil
1 tsp sugar (optional)
250ml (½ pint; 1 cup) water

Preheat the oven to 160°C (325°F), Gas Mark 3.

Mix all the ingredients together and form into a firm dough. Cut into individual scones with a pastry cutter or make one large scone, cutting a cross on the top. Bake for 10 to 15 minutes according to size.

Rye bread

450g (1lb; 4 cups) rye flour
½ tsp salt
40g (1½oz) fresh yeast
1 tsp raw cane molasses sugar
1 tsp caraway seeds
250ml (½ pint; 1 cup) warm water

Mix the yeast with the sugar and pour on half the water. Leave for 5 to 10 minutes until frothy.

Add the salt to the flour and pour in the yeast mixture. Add the caraway seeds and the remaining water and mix to a dough. Knead for 5 to 10 minutes and then leave covered in a warm place until the dough has doubled in size. Knock back (pat the dough until it is almost back to its original size) and knead again for 2 or 3 minutes. Form the dough into two round loaves and place on a well-greased baking tray. Cover and leave for 30 minutes until well risen. Preheat the oven to 200°C (400°F), Gas Mark 6.

Bake the loaves for 10 minutes, then reduce the oven setting to 180°C (350°F), Gas Mark 4 and bake for a further 25 minutes.

Russian-style rye bread can be made with just rye flour, water and salt. Wholemeal wheat or spelt wheat bread can be made by following the above recipe but using wheat flour instead of rye and reducing the quantity of yeast to 25g (1oz). Omit the caraway seeds and use cashew nuts or a few wheat flakes instead. Sprinkle with sesame seeds, poppy seeds or wheat flakes.

Carrot and fig slice

175g (6oz; 1½ cups) wholewheat flour
175g (6oz; 1½ cups) grated carrot
175g (6oz; 1½ cups) dried figs
75ml (3fl oz; ½ cup) sesame oil
½ tsp aniseed

Preheat the oven to 160°C (325°F), Gas Mark 3.

Place the figs in a saucepan, cover with water and cook for 20 minutes. Drain and liquidize to a purée.

Mix the purée with the rest of the ingredients. Spoon the mixture into a well-greased or lined 18cm (7in) baking tin and bake for 1 hour.

Allow to cool before turning out.

Orange and cashew nut crunchies

225g (8oz; 2 cups) wholemeal flour
125g (4oz; 1 cup) ground cashew nuts
125g (4oz; ½ cup) raw cane sugar or barley malt
grated zest of 1 orange
4 tbsp sesame oil

Preheat the oven to 170°C (335°F), Gas Mark 3.

Warm the oil and sugar or barley malt in a saucepan for 2 to 3 minutes. Mix with the dry ingredients and spoon into a well-greased swiss roll tin. Bake for 15 to 20 minutes. Allow to cool before cutting into fingers or squares.

Drinks and miscellaneous

Cashew nut milk

125g (4oz; 1 cup) cashew nuts
1 litre (1¾ pints; 4 cups) water
1 tbsp barley malt (optional)

Grind the cashew nuts to a fine powder in a liquidizer. Add some of the water and barley malt and liquidize until smooth. Gradually add the remaining water. Keep chilled.

Cashew nut cream

Follow the above recipe, reducing the amount of water to 125ml (¼ pint; ½ cup). Serve with fruit or puddings.

Carrot and cashew nut spread

125g (4oz; 1 cup) carrots, cooked and puréed
125g (4oz; 1 cup) cashew nuts, ground
1 tbsp fresh parsley, finely chopped
pinch of sea salt or 1 tsp barley miso
sesame oil (optional)

Mix the ingredients together, adding a little sesame oil to bind the mixture if necessary.

Mushroom and tahini spread

125g (4oz; 2 cups) mushrooms, sliced
2 tbsp tahini
1 tbsp lemon juice
1 tsp barley miso
1 tbsp fresh parsley finely chopped
1 tbsp sesame oil

Cook the mushrooms in the sesame oil until soft. Liquidize to a purée and mix well with the remaining ingredients.

Lemon and orange barley water

50g (2oz; ¼ cup) pot barley
1 litre (1¾ pints; 4 cups) water
2 oranges
1 lemon
2 tbsp barley malt

Place the barley in a saucepan with the water. Bring to the boil and simmer for one hour. Stir in the barley malt and leave to cool.

Wash the fruit and grate the rinds into a jug. Cut away and discard the pith. Thinly slice the flesh and add to the rind.

Strain the barley water and pour into the jug with the fruit.

Lemon and elderflower cordial

*Use freshly gathered elderflowers or dried elderflowers bought
  from a healthfood store.*
10 elderflower heads or 25g (1oz; ¼ cup) dried elderflowers
1 litre (1¾ pints; 4 cups) boiling water
zest and juice of 2 lemons
lemon slices
2 tbsp raw cane sugar

Place the lemon zest, elderflowers and sugar in a saucepan
and pour on the boiling water. Leave for 10 to 20 minutes and
strain off the juice. Add the fresh lemon juice and serve
chilled with slices of lemon. Dilute to taste.

Elderberry punch

*Gather the elderberries in the early autumn and freeze some for
  later use.*
900g (2lb; 8 cups) elderberries
½ litre (1 pint; 2 cups) water
1 litre (1¾ pints; 4 cups) orange juice
zest and juice of 2 lemons
½ tbsp cane sugar (or to taste)
2 oranges, sliced
½ litre (1 pint; 2 cups) green leaf tea, strained
2 tbsp grenadine (optional)

Place the elderberries in a large saucepan with the water and
lemon zest and bring to the boil. Simmer for 10 minutes
and then strain off the pulp. Pour the elderberry juice back
into the saucepan and add the orange juice, lemon juice, tea
and grenadine. Add sugar to taste. Bring to the boil and then
simmer for 10 minutes. Place slices of orange in a jug and
pour on the punch. Serve hot.

On Day 2 this may be served either chilled or hot with two
sticks of cinnamon and a few sprigs of thyme.

Day 2

The following foods can be eaten:

Cereals, grains and flour   Maize flour, cornflour, corn pasta, sorghum, arrowroot, oats, oatmeal, oat cakes, quinoa, quinoa flour, green banana flour.

Meat   Pork, wild boar, venison.

Nuts and seeds   Brazil nuts and spread, tiger nuts, macadamia nuts, pine nuts, pumpkin seeds, hemp seeds.

Sugars   Fruit sugar, corn syrup, oat syrup.

Drinks   Mint tea, thyme tea, sage tea, lemon verbena and lemon balm tea, blackcurrant leaf tea, hibiscus tea.

Vegetables   Avocado pear, cucumber, marrow, pumpkin, zucchini, okra, plantain, potato, tomato, aubergine, peppers, onion, leek, garlic, asparagus, sweetcorn.

Herbs and spices   Cayenne pepper, paprika pepper, ginger, turmeric, cardamom, cinnamon, bay, mint, basil, sage, oregano, thyme, rosemary, lemon balm, chives.

Fruit   Banana, melon, kiwi fruit, currants, gooseberries, cape gooseberries, pineapple.

Oils   Virgin olive oil, flax seed oil, hemp seed oil.

Breakfast

Melon salad
Oat flake muesli
Old-fashioned oatmeal porridge
Speedy oat porridge
Sorghum porridge
Polenta

Soups and starters

Baked tomato soup
Potato and onion soup
Asparagus soup
Avocado and green pepper soup
Spiced pumpkin and ginger soup
Gazpacho
Tortillas with sweetcorn and tomato filling
Avocado and zucchini dip
Stuffed tomatoes
Venison and pine nut ramekins

Main meals

Pork and pineapple kebabs
Roast pork/wild boar with juniper
Pigs' liver and onions
Venison goulash
Venison and cucumber stir-fry
Meatballs in tomato and pepper sauce

Vegetarian main meals

Polenta with tomato and pepper sauce
Leek and potato bake
Green pepper and aubergine flan
Quinoa pilaff
Brazil nut roast

Vegetables and salads

Black olive and tomato salad
Cucumber, avocado and asparagus salad
Baked plantains
Greek-style onions
Baked vegetables

Puddings and desserts

Pineapple upside-down cake
Gooseberry crumble
Grilled pineapple with macadamia nuts
Fruit crêpes
Blackcurrant sorbet

Cakes and biscuits

Green banana and oatmeal scones
Hemp seed bread
Banana flapjacks
Oatcake biscuits
Brazil nut cookies
Ginger fork biscuits

Drinks and miscellaneous

Tiger nut milk
Oat milk (1)
Oat milk (2)
Hemp seed milk
Pineapple crush
Banana milkshake
Brazil nut butter
Hemp seed butter

Breakfasts

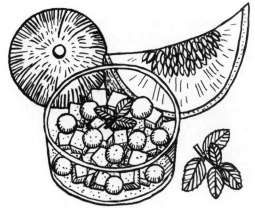

Melon salad

1 cantaloupe melon
1 honeydew melon
1 tsp ground ginger (optional)
1 tsp fruit sugar (optional)
4 sprigs of mint.

Cut the melons in half and scoop out balls of flesh with a melon scoop or cut the flesh into squares. Place a mixture of the two types of melon in glass bowls. Mix the ginger and fruit sugar together and sprinkle on top of the melon. Garnish with sprigs of mint.

Oat flake muesli

2 cups jumbo oat flakes
½ cup oat bran and germ (optional)
chopped brazil nuts
pumpkin seeds
fresh or sun-dried bananas

Mix together and serve with pineapple juice, stewed gooseberries or tiger nut milk.

Old-fashioned oatmeal porridge

(Serves 2–3)
1 cup pinhead oatmeal or whole oat groats
4 cups water
pinch of salt

Place the oats in a saucepan (use a double-boiler if available), add the cold water and bring to the boil. Turn off the heat and leave overnight.

Next morning, bring to the boil again and simmer for 30 minutes, stirring from time to time.

Speedy oat porridge

(Serves 2)
1 cup organic rolled oat flakes
4 cups water

Place the oats in a saucepan and add the cold water. Bring to the boil and simmer for 1 minute, stirring as it thickens.

Sorghum porridge

(Serves 2)
1 cup sorghum meal
4 cups water
pinch of salt

Cook as for oat flake porridge, stirring all the time.

Polenta (maize meal)

225g (8oz; 2 cups) fine maize meal (polenta)
500ml (1 pint; 2 cups) water
1 tsp sea salt

Bring the salted water to the boil in a heavy-based saucepan, and gradually add the polenta, stirring with a wooden spoon to keep it smooth. Cook gently for 20 minutes until it thickens and comes cleanly away from the sides of the pan.

Pour into a well-oiled, shallow baking dish, approximately 20 x 31cm (8 x 12in). Spread out with a wet spatula so that the polenta is roughly 1cm (½in) thick. Leave to set and then cut into pieces and serve.

This is a traditional northern Italian dish used instead of pasta or bread, enjoyed hot or cold, sweet or savoury. Polenta blends well with meat, game and fish dishes and vegetables. It may also be served with sweet and savory sauces and is often served on its own.

Soups and starters

How to peel and de-seed tomatoes

Bring a small pan of water to the boil. Score an 'x' on the base of each tomato and immerse in the water until the skin starts to split. Transfer immediately to a pan of cold water and peel off the skin with the aid of a small knife. Cut the tomatoes in half crossways and squeeze out the seeds. Chop as required.

Baked tomato soup

750g (1½lb; 6 cups) tomatoes
1 onion, sliced
2 cloves garlic
2 tbsp freshly chopped basil
1 litre (1¾ pints; 4 cups) pork stock or water
sea salt

Preheat the oven to 180°C (350°F), Gas Mark 4.

Cut the tomatoes into halves and scoop out the seeds. Place on a baking tray with the onion and garlic cloves and bake for

20 minutes. Remove from the oven and take the skins off the
tomatoes. Allow to cool slightly and then liquidize all the
vegetables.

Bring the stock to the boil and add the baked ingredients,
together with the basil and salt. Cook for 5 minutes and serve
with a sprinkling of basil.

Potato and onion soup

450g (1lb; 4 cups) potatoes, peeled and diced
2 onions, diced
1 litre (1¾ pints; 4 cups) pork stock or water
2 bay leaves
bunch of chives, chopped
sprig of rosemary
sea salt

Place all the ingredients, except for the salt and the chives,
in a saucepan and cook in half the quantity of water/stock for
20 minutes. Allow the liquid to cool slightly, and then blend
in a liquidizer. Add the salt, the remaining stock and the
chopped chives and reheat gently. Cook for a further 5
minutes and serve.

Asparagus soup

450g (1lb) asparagus
1 litre (1¾ pints; 4 cups) pork or vegetable stock or water
1 large onion, sliced
1 tbsp chopped mint
1 sprig lemon verbena (optional)
sea salt

Wash and prepare the asparagus. Cut off the tips and trim off
the coarse outer parts of the remaining stems. Cut into 2cm
(1in) pieces.

Cook the tips in a little water and then drain off, reserving
the water. The tips are not needed in this recipe and could be
used in a salad such as the Cucumber, Avocado and Asparagus
Salad on page 69. Use this water to cook the onion and
asparagus stems. Add the lemon verbena, salt and more liquid

if necessary, and cook for 5 to 10 minutes until the asparagus stems are tender. Remove the lemon verbena sprig.

Liquidize the soup to a creamy consistency and return to the saucepan to reheat, adding the remaining stock. Serve with a sprinkling of chopped mint.

Avocado and green pepper soup

2 large avocado pears
2 green peppers, de-seeded and chopped
1 litre (1¾ pints; 4 cups) stock or water
2 bay leaves
sea salt
freshly chopped mint

Cook the peppers in a little of the stock with the bay leaves and a pinch of salt until tender. Remove the bay leaves.

Peel and stone the avocados and place the flesh in a liquidizer with the peppers. Blend to a purée and return to the saucepan to reheat, adding the remaining stock. Serve with a sprinkling of chopped mint.

Spiced pumpkin and ginger soup

900g (2lb; 8 cups) pumpkin or squash flesh, diced
1 litre (1¾ pints; 4 cups) stock or water
1 tsp root ginger, grated
2 cloves garlic, crushed
1 dried chilli, crushed
1 tsp ground turmeric
sea salt

Place the pumpkin in a large saucepan and add the grated ginger, garlic, salt and spices. Cover with some of the water/stock and bring to the boil. Simmer for 10 minutes, then allow to cool slightly.

Place the contents of the pan in a liquidizer and blend until smooth. Return to the saucepan, add the remaining stock and cook for a further 5 minutes.

Garlic and ginger may be prepared in larger quantities and frozen in small portions.

Gazpacho

450g (1lb; 4 cups) tomatoes peeled, de-seeded and chopped
2 onions, chopped
1 large cucumber, peeled and diced
1 large green pepper, de-seeded and diced
2 cloves garlic, crushed
250ml (½ pint; 1 cup) stock or water
4 tbsp olive oil
paprika, pepper

Place half the tomatoes, stock, garlic, black pepper and olive oil in a liquidizer and blend to a purée. Mix with the vegetables and refrigerate for 2 to 4 hours before serving.

This soup is ideal for a hot summer's day.

Tortillas with sweetcorn and tomato filling

FOR THE FILLING:
225g (8oz; 2 cups) cooked sweetcorn
4 tomatoes, skinned and chopped
1 tbsp tomato purée
1 onion, chopped
2 cloves garlic, crushed
2 tsp fresh oregano
sea salt
FOR THE TORTILLAS:
175g (6oz; 1½ cups) maize flour
250ml (½ pint; 1 cup) warm water
½ tsp sea salt

Cook the onion and garlic in a little water until soft. Add the tomatoes and sweetcorn and cook for another 5 minutes. Mix in the tomato purée and seasoning.

Put the maize flour and salt in a bowl and gradually beat in the water and oil. Knead until a smooth, elastic dough is formed. Divide into eight portions and roll out each one between two sheets of greaseproof paper or tough polythene to form a thin round about 15cm (6in) in diameter. Dry-fry or cook on a hot griddle for 2 or 3 minutes on each side.

Spoon two or three tablespoons of filling into each tortilla, fold over and keep warm on a serving dish.

Avocado may be used instead of sweetcorn.

Avocado and zucchini dip

2 large ripe avocado pears
2 cloves garlic, crushed
125g (4oz; 1 cup) cooked zucchini
sea salt
paprika pepper
FOR THE CRUDITÉS:
red, yellow and green pepper, cut lengthways
cucumber, cut lengthways
baby corn

Halve the avocados and remove the stones. Scoop out the flesh and mash together with the cooked zucchini, garlic and seasoning. Serve with crudités or tortillas.

Stuffed tomatoes

4 large tomatoes
125g (4oz; ½ cup) quinoa, cooked
50g (2oz; ½ cup) pumpkin seeds, dry roasted and chopped
50g (2oz; ½ cup) brazil nuts, finely chopped
1 large onion, chopped and fried
1 clove garlic, crushed
1 tbsp freshly chopped herbs (basil, thyme or marjoram)
sea salt

Preheat the oven to 160°C (325°F), Gas Mark 3.

Cut the tops off the tomatoes and scoop out all the flesh. Discard the seeds and chop the flesh. Mix with the remaining ingredients and spoon back into the tomato shells. Bake for 20 minutes.

This stuffing may also be used for stuffing marrow, zucchini, aubergine and peppers. The cooking time may vary.

Venison and pine nut ramekins

275g (10oz) minced raw venison
1 onion, chopped
250ml (½ pint; 1 cup) stock
2 bay leaves
sea salt
1 tbsp cornflour
50g (2oz; ½ cup) pine nuts, chopped

Bring the stock to the boil and add the onion, minced venison, salt and bay leaves, and cook for 15 minutes. Remove the bay leaves.

Mix the cornflour with a little cold water and stir into the mixture. Continue to cook, stirring until the mixture thickens. Pour into four well-oiled ramekin dishes and sprinkle with the chopped pine nuts. Place under the grill long enough to brown the tops lightly.

Main meals

Pork and pineapple kebabs

675g (1½lb) lean organic pork, cut into 2.5cm (1in) cubes
1 pineapple, skinned and cut into cubes
2 green peppers, cut into 2.5cm (1in) pieces
8 bay leaves
2 tsp freshly chopped thyme
sea salt

Thread the pork, pineapple, pepper and bay leaves onto four long skewers. Sprinkle the kebabs with thyme and salt and place on an oiled grill rack. Grill under a medium heat for 10 to 15 minutes, turning frequently.

Roast pork/wild boar with juniper

1kg (2.2lb) boned loin of organically reared pork/wild boar
10 juniper berries, crushed
2 cloves garlic, crushed
1 tbsp fine oatmeal
2 tbsp freshly chopped sage
sea salt

Preheat the oven to 180°C (350°F), Gas Mark 4.

Mix together the juniper berries, garlic, oatmeal, sage and salt.

Trim off the skin and excess fat from the pork and cut some deep slashes in the top and sides. Place in a roasting tray and cover with the oatmeal and juniper mixture. Roast for approximately 1 hour until thoroughly cooked.

Pigs' liver and onions

450g (1lb) organic pig's liver, thinly sliced
3 onions, sliced
1 tbsp fine oatmeal
2 tbsp olive oil
250ml (½ pint; 1 cup) pork or vegetable stock or water
1 tsp cornflour
sea salt

Warm the oil with a little water in a heavy-based frying pan. Cool-fry the onions until transparent and place on a serving dish and keep warm.

Roll the slices of liver in the oatmeal seasoned with salt, and gently cool-fry on both sides for 2 or 3 minutes until just cooked. Place on top of the onions.

Pour the stock into the pan, adding a little cornflour mixed with cold water to thicken if necessary, and then heat to make a gravy.

Venison goulash

450g (1lb) venison, cut into cubes
1 large onion, sliced
1 zucchini, sliced
1 green pepper, de-seeded and chopped
250ml (½ pint; 1 cup) water
450g (1lb; 4 cups) tomatoes skinned and chopped
225g (8oz; 2 cups) sweetcorn kernels
1 tbsp cornflour
basil, thyme or rosemary
sea salt

Bring the water to the boil and add the venison. Cook for 2 or 3 minutes to seal, then add the vegetables, herbs and seasoning. Cover and cook for 40 minutes.

Mix the cornflour with a little cold water and stir into the goulash to thicken the sauce.

Venison and cucumber stir-fry

450g (1lb) lean venison, cut into thin strips
2 cloves garlic
1 tsp grated ginger
½ cucumber, halved lengthways and sliced
225g (8oz; 2 cups) baby sweetcorn
1 red pepper, cut into strips
sea salt

Heat a little water in a large frying pan or wok. Add the venison and cook for 5 minutes. Add the rest of the ingredients, leaving the cucumber until the end.

Meatballs in tomato and pepper sauce

450g (1lb) minced meat (pork or venison)
1 large onion, chopped and fried
2 cloves garlic, crushed
2 tbsp tomato purée
2 tbsp fine oatmeal or maize meal
1 tsp grated ginger
½ tsp ground cardamom
½ tsp chilli powder (optional)

sea salt
250ml (½ pint; 1 cup) stock
tomato and pepper sauce (see below)

Prepare the tomato sauce by following the recipe below and adding 450ml (¾ pint) stock or water.

Mix all the ingredients together, either by hand or in a food mixer, then mould into eight meatballs. Bring the stock to the boil and add the tomato sauce and the meatballs. Simmer gently for 30 minutes.

Vegetarian main meals

Polenta with tomato and pepper sauce

6 fresh tomatoes, skinned and chopped
1 pepper, de-seeded and diced
2 spring onions, chopped
1 clove garlic, crushed
1 tsp basil
½ tsp cayenne pepper
sea salt
polenta (see page 56)

Prepare the polenta by following the recipe on page 56 and keep warm.

Cook the vegetables in a little water for 15 minutes until tender. Rub through a sieve or leave chunky, then season.

Cut the polenta into 5cm (2in) squares. Serve hot with the tomato sauce.

Leek and potato bake

675g (1½lb; 6 cups) potatoes, thinly sliced
275g (10oz; 2½ cups) leeks, sliced
2 cloves garlic, crushed
sea salt
250ml (½ pint; 1 cup) vegetable stock

Preheat the oven to 160°C (325°F), Gas Mark 3.

Grease a shallow ovenproof baking dish and arrange the sliced potatoes and leeks in layers, sprinkling each layer with salt and ending with a potato layer on the top. Add the garlic to the stock and pour over. Bake for 1 to 1½ hours until the potatoes are tender.

Green pepper and aubergine flan

FOR THE PASTRY CASE:
125g (4oz; 1 cup) fine oatmeal
175g (6oz; 1½ cups) mashed potato
125ml (¼ pint; ½ cup) olive oil
pinch of salt
water to mix
FOR THE FILLING:
2 aubergines, thinly sliced
2 green peppers, thinly sliced
sea salt
FOR THE SAUCE:
1 onion, finely chopped
250ml (½ pint; 1 cup) vegetable stock or water
1 tbsp cornflour
1 tbsp freshly chopped basil
sea salt

Preheat the oven to 160°C (325°F), Gas Mark 3.

To prepare the flan case, mix the ingredients together using a little cold water to make a firm dough. Roll out between two sheets of greaseproof paper or tough polythene and mould the pastry into the flan dish.

Sprinkle the sliced aubergines with salt and leave for 30 minutes to remove the bitterness. Rinse, drain and dry on kitchen paper. Steam or boil the aubergines in a little water for 3 to 5 minutes until just tender, then arrange them in the flan case with the green pepper.

For the sauce, bring the stock/water to the boil and cook the onion until soft. Mix the cornflour with a little cold water and stir into the stock to thicken the sauce. Add the basil and salt and pour into the flan case. Bake for 40 minutes.

Quinoa pilaff

225g (8oz; 1 cup) quinoa
1 litre (1¾ pints; 4 cups) water
1 red pepper, de-seeded and chopped
1 green pepper, de-seeded and chopped
125g (4oz; 1 cup) okra, sliced
125g (4oz; 1 cup) fresh pineapple chunks
bunch of spring onions
2 cloves garlic, crushed
1 tsp grated ginger
½ tsp paprika pepper
sea salt
2 tbsp olive oil
FOR SERVING:
2–4 plantains or bananas

Toast the quinoa in a dry saucepan over a moderate heat until the grains are lightly browned and some begin to pop. Leave to one side.

Warm the oil and a little water in a pan and gently cool-fry the onions, garlic and ginger for 2 to 3 minutes. Add the peppers, okra and pineapple chunks and cook for a further 5 minutes. Add the quinoa, water and salt, cover and bring to the boil. Simmer for 15 to 20 minutes until all the water is absorbed. Sprinkle with paprika pepper and serve with sliced cooked plantains or fresh bananas.

To cook the plantains, cut in half lengthways without peeling. Score the skin through to the flesh in a few places. Put in a pan, cover with water and bring to the boil. Simmer for 20 minutes, Drain, then peel and cut each plantain lengthways into two or three slices.

Brazil nut roast

175g (6oz; 1½ cups) quinoa flour
50g (2oz; ½ cup) oat flakes
175g (6oz; 1½ cups) brazil nuts, chopped
175g (6oz; 1½ cups) zucchini, grated
2 onions, finely chopped
250ml (½ pint; 1 cup) water
1 tbsp freshly chopped sage
sea salt
1 tbsp olive oil

Preheat the oven to 160°C (325°F), Gas Mark 3.

Line a 1kg (2lb) loaf tin with greaseproof paper.

Mix all the ingredients together, adding more water to bind if necessary, and turn into the tin. Bake for 1 hour until firm to the touch.

This recipe may also be used to make burgers and stuffing.

Vegetables and salads

Black olive and tomato salad

4 large marmade tomatoes
1 red onion (optional)
125g (4oz; 1 cup) black olives
2 tbsp virgin olive oil
sea salt
black pepper
1 tbsp freshly chopped basil

Cut the tomatoes crossways into thin slices using a serrated knife. Arrange them in a dish, alternating with a few slices of onion. Add the olives and sprinkle on the olive oil, seasoning and chopped basil.

Cucumber, avocado and asparagus salad

1 cucumber, cut into chunks
2 avocados
125g (4oz; 1 cup) asparagus tips
paprika pepper
sprig of mint

Cook the asparagus tips in a little water until just tender. Drain and allow to cool. (The stalks may be used in soup.)

Skin and stone the avocados, then cut the flesh into chunks. Mix with the cucumber and asparagus and sprinkle with paprika pepper. Garnish with mint.

Baked plantains

4 medium plantains

Plantains are a variety of banana which are larger than ordinary bananas and usually green in colour. They are sold in West Indian stores and some supermarkets.

Preheat the oven to 160°C (325°F), Gas Mark 3.

Bake the plantains in their skins for about 30 minutes and serve hot.

Greek-style onions

675g (1½lb; 6 cups) small pickling onions
1 tbsp olive oil
2 tsp tomato purée
250ml (½ pint; 1 cup) stock or water
sea salt
sprig of fresh thyme

Blanch the onions in boiling water for 1 minute only, then drain and rinse in cold water. Remove the skins with a small knife or your fingers.

Place the onions in a heavy-based saucepan with the stock,

oil, tomato purée, thyme and salt. Bring to the boil and simmer gently for 30 minutes. Remove the sprig of thyme and serve hot.

Baked vegetables

1 red pepper, de-seeded and halved
1 green pepper, de-seeded and halved
1 large onion, skinned and quartered
6 whole cloves of garlic, skinned
3–4 zucchinis, sliced lengthways
6–8 cherry tomatoes
1 bunch of asparagus, trimmed
herbs for garnishing (mint, basil, chives, oregano)
2 tbsp olive oil or dripping
sea salt

Preheat the oven to 160°C (325°F), Gas Mark 3.

Place the vegetables in a greased roasting pan and bake for 30 minutes. Sprinkle with salt and any herbs of your choice and serve hot.

Puddings and desserts

Pineapple upside-down cake

1 pineapple, skinned and sliced
175g (6oz; 1½ cups) maize flour
175g (6oz; 1½ cups) cornflour
125g (4oz; ½ cup) corn syrup

125ml (¼ pint; ½ cup) olive oil
2 cups water
1 tsp bicarbonate of soda
1 tsp cream of tartar

Preheat the oven to 160°C (325°F), Gas Mark 3.

Put the sliced pineapple into the bottom of a well-oiled ovenproof dish. Mix together the other ingredients and spoon over the fruit, pressing down well. Cook for approximately 45 minutes until firm.

Gooseberry crumble

675g (1½lb; 6 cups) gooseberries
125g (4oz; 1 cup) fine oatmeal
125g (4oz; 1 cup) oat flakes
125g (4oz; ½ cup) fruit sugar
125ml (¼ pint; ½ cup) olive oil

Preheat the oven to 160°C (325°F), Gas Mark 3.

Top and tail the gooseberries and cook with a little water until just beginning to soften. Pour into an ovenproof dish, adding a little fruit sugar to sweeten if necessary.

Place the other ingredients in a large bowl and lightly crumble with your fingers. Place on top of the fruit and bake for 30 minutes.

Grilled pineapple with macadamia nuts

1 large pineapple
1 tbsp fruit sugar
50g (2oz; ½ cup) macadamia nuts, sliced

Using a serrated knife, trim off about 1cm (½in) from each end of the pineapple, saving some of the leaves.

Cut the pineapple into quarters lengthways and carefully trim away the core. Then cut along the base of each quarter so that the flesh is separated from the skin. Cut the flesh in half lengthways and then into four crossways to give bite-size portions.

Sprinkle each quarter with fruit sugar and place under a grill until just beginning to caramelize. Decorate with macadamia nuts and serve.

Fruit crêpes

125g (4oz; 1 cup) fine oatmeal, maize or quinoa flour
50g (2oz; ½ cup) cornflour or green banana flour
250ml (½ pint; 1 cup) nut milk or water
1 tsp fruit sugar
fruit of your choice

Place all the dry ingredients in a bowl and add half the liquid.
Beat well to form a smooth, thick batter. Gradually add the
remaining liquid to produce a pouring consistency. Spoon two
or three tablespoons of the mixture onto a hot griddle and
cook on both sides until just golden.

Serve hot with a fruit filling of your choice.

Blackcurrant sorbet

900g (2lb; 8 cups) blackcurrants
125g (4oz; ½ cup) fruit sugar
1 litre (1¾ pints; 4 cups) water
sprig of lemon balm (optional)

Cook the blackcurrants with the sugar, lemon balm and water.
Mash and sieve. Discard the pulp. Pour the blackcurrant
syrup into a shallow container and freeze until mushy. Whisk
until light and fluffy. Leave in the freezer until firm.

Cakes and biscuits

Green banana and oatmeal scones

125g (4oz; 1 cup) green banana flour
125g (4oz; 1 cup) fine oatmeal
2 tbsp olive oil
25g (1oz; ⅛ cup) fruit sugar
1 tsp bicarbonate of soda
250ml (½ pint; 1 cup) nut milk or water

Preheat the oven to 160°C (325°F), Gas Mark 3.

Place the dry ingredients in a large bowl and rub in the oil. Add sufficient liquid and mix to form a firm dough. Roll out to about 2cm (¾in) thickness and cut into rounds with a 5cm (2in) cutter. Place on a baking tray and cook for 20 minutes.

Hemp seed bread

125g (4oz; 1 cup) quinoa or potato flour
125g (4oz; 1 cup) fine oatmeal
75g (3oz; ¾ cup) ground hemp seeds
1 tsp bicarbonate of soda
pinch of salt
1 cup water

Preheat the oven to 180°C (350°F), Gas Mark 4.

Mix the ingredients together with sufficient water to make a firm dough. Place the dough in a lined 1lb loaf tin and bake for 40 minutes.

Banana flapjacks

125g (4oz; 1 cup) oat flakes
1 large banana, mashed
2 tbsp corn syrup
3 tbsp olive oil
½ tsp ginger

Preheat the oven to 160°C (325°F), Gas Mark 3.

Place the corn syrup and oil in a saucepan and heat gently for 1 minute. Add the oats, ginger and mashed banana and mix thoroughly. Place the mixture in a well-greased swiss roll tin, pressing well in. Bake for 35 minutes until golden.

Leave the flapjacks to cool in the tin for 15 minutes before marking into fingers.

Oatcake biscuits

225g (8oz; 2 cups) fine or medium oatmeal
1 tbsp pork dripping or olive oil, warmed
½ tsp bicarbonate of soda
pinch of salt
3–5 tbsp boiling water

Preheat the oven to 160°C (325°F), Gas Mark 3.

Mix the dry ingredients together in a large bowl. Make a well in the centre and pour in the warm dripping or oil. Stir in enough boiling water to make a firm dough.

Knead the dough on a surface dusted with oatmeal and divide into two. Quickly roll out each half into a 20cm (8in) circle, approximately ½cm (¼in) in thickness and cut into quarters. Place on a well-greased baking tray and bake for 25 to 30 minutes until firm but not brown.

Brazil nut cookies

125g (4oz; 1 cup) fine oatmeal
50g (2oz; ½ cup) oat flakes
125g (4oz; 1 cup) Brazil nuts, finely chopped
75g (3oz; ⅓ cup) fruit sugar
4 tbsp olive oil
1 tsp arrowroot
water to mix

Preheat the oven to 160°C (325°F), Gas Mark 3.

Place all the dry ingredients in a large mixing bowl and rub in the oil. Add sufficient water to make a firm dough. Roll out the dough on a surface dusted with arrowroot or cornflour and cut into individual cookies with a biscuit cutter. Place the cookies on a greased baking sheet and cook for 10 to 15 minutes until light golden in colour.

Ginger fork biscuits

125g (4oz; 1 cup) maize flour
125g (4oz; 1 cup) green banana flour
2 tbsp corn syrup
4 tbsp olive oil
1 tsp ground ginger
1 tsp ground cinnamon
water to mix

Preheat the oven to 160°C (325°F), Gas Mark 3.

Mix the ingredients together in a bowl, adding sufficient water to form a firm dough. Divide the dough into pieces the size of a walnut and roll into balls. Place on a greased baking sheet and flatten with a fork. Bake for 10 to 15 minutes. Leave the biscuits on the baking sheet to firm before lifting them onto a wire rack to cool.

Drinks and miscellaneous

Tiger nut milk

225g (8oz; 1⅓ cups) tiger nuts, washed and soaked overnight
1 litre (1¾ pints; 4 cups) water

Rinse the tiger nuts. Liquidize with the water and strain off the pulp. Use the milk to pour over cereal. Discard the pulp or use in recipes.

Oat milk (1)

50g (2oz; ½ cup) pinhead oatmeal or groats
500ml (1 pint; 2 cups) water

Rinse the groats and leave to soak in the water overnight. Liquidize the next day and pour through a fine sieve. Discard the pulp or use in recipes. Serve cold.

Oat milk (2)

50g (2oz; ½ cup) oatmeal or flakes
1 litre (1¾ pints; 4 cups) water
1 tsp fruit sugar (optional)
drop of natural vanilla essence (optional)

Place the oats in a large pan with the water and bring to the boil. Simmer for 10 minutes. Allow the oats to cool slightly, then liquidize until smooth and strain. Serve hot or cold. Oat milk makes a particularly delicious and warming drink served hot with a little sweetener and vanilla essence for flavouring.

Hemp seed milk

125g (4oz; 1 cup) hemp seeds, soaked for 48 hours
1 litre (1¾ pints; 4 cups) water

Place the seeds in a pan with the water and bring to the boil. Simmer for 15 to 20 minutes. Remove the pan from the heat as soon as a yellow film starts to form on the surface. Leave the liquid to cool for a few minutes and then pour through a fine strainer or coffee filter. Serve chilled.

Pineapple crush

1 pineapple
500ml–1 litre (1–1¾ pints) water
½ tsp fresh ginger

Method 1: remove the rind from the pineapple using a serrated knife. Cut the flesh into chunks and liquidize with ½ litre to 1 litre of water.
Method 2: place the pineapple chunks in a pan with the fresh ginger, cover with water and bring to the boil. Simmer for 5 to 7 minutes until tender, allow to cool slightly and liquidize until smooth. Serve hot or cold.

Banana milkshake

1 peeled banana
½ litre (1 pint; 2 cups) nut or oat milk

Place the ingredients in a liquidizer and blend until smooth. Serve immediately.

Brazil nut butter

Wash the nuts and leave to soak overnight. Rinse off the water and then liquidize, dropping the nuts one by one onto the rotary blades of the blender. Add a little virgin olive oil to make a smooth paste. Eat immediately or freeze.

Hemp seed butter

Follow the recipe for brazil nut butter but soak the hemp
seeds for 48 hours before liquidizing. Alternatively, the seeds
could also be lightly toasted using a dry frying pan and
removing from the heat the moment they begin to pop.
Liquidize and add a little virgin olive oil. Serve immediately
or freeze.

Day 3

The following foods can be eaten:

Cereals, grains and flour   Brown rice, brown rice flour and
    bran, rice pasta, rice cakes, rice biscuits, wild rice, sago,
    sago flour, soya flour, lentil flour, gram flour (chickpea),
    any other pulse flour, cream of tartar.

Meat, etc   Chicken and eggs, duck and eggs, quail and eggs,
    turkey, pigeon and any other game bird, tofu, tempeh, rice
    or soya miso, umeboshi plum dressing, tamari soya sauce.

Nuts and seeds   Coconut, almonds, sunflower seeds, (not
    peanuts).

Sugars   Honey, rice syrup, date syrup, beet sugar.

Drinks   Chicory coffee, dandelion root coffee, rooibosch tea,
    soya milk, cocoa, carob, camomile tea, grape juice.

Vegetables   The aster family (lettuce, chicory, endive, globe
    and Jerusalem artichoke, salsify, sunflower seed sprouts);
    the beet family (beetroot, spinach, Swiss chard); the pea
    family (peas, mangetout, sugar peas, broad beans, runner
    beans, French beans, pulses including dried beans, lentils,
    chickpeas, lima beans and soya beans)

Herbs and spices   Tarragon, fenugreek seeds, nutmeg,
    liquorice, senna, red clover.

Fruit   Peach, plum, damson, apricot, cherry, nectarine,
    prune, Cape gooseberries, dates, grapes, raisins.

Oils, etc   Sunflower, safflower, soya and almond oils,
    tropical oils – coconut or palm oil if available, wine vinegar,
    balsamic vinegar.

Breakfasts

Fresh fruit salad
Compote of apricots and peaches
Rice porridge with prunes or hunza apricots
Rice pancakes with apricot or plum purée
Rice flake muesli

Soups and starters

Cream of cannellini and almond soup
Lettuce and tarragon soup
Spinach and egg-drop soup
Green pea soup
Bean sprout and noodle soup
Stuffed vine leaves (dolmas)
Spinach and tofu puffs
Almond and date stuffed peaches
Chicken liver pâté
Stuffed artichokes

Main meals

Pigeon with prunes
Turkey and apricot pilaff
Stir-fry duck with mangetout
Pot-roast pheasant/game bird
Chicken with beetroot
Roast chicken with plum stuffing

Vegetarian main meals

Artichoke and three bean casserole
Spinach and lentil flan
Tempeh or tofu stir-fry
Aduki bean burgers
Spinach roulade with chickpea and salsify filling

Vegetables and salads

Cherry and almond salad
Beetroot and chicory salad
Green bean salad
Roasted Jerusalem artichokes
Egg mayonnaise
Tofu mayonnaise

Puddings and desserts

Damson syllabub
Chicory coffee ice cream
Apricot and almond flan

Cakes and biscuits

Carob and coconut brownies
Sticky prune cake
Rich fruit cake
Chocolate almond cookies
Cherry and coconut slices
Almond nougat
Rice bread
Raisin bun loaf

Drinks and miscellaneous

Rice milk
Soya milk (1)
Soya milk (2)
Honey egg-nog
Hot chocolate
Peach cocktail
Almond and sunflower seed nut butters

Breakfast

Fresh fruit salad

250ml (½ pint; 1 cup) white grape juice
2 white nectarines, cut into segments
2 yellow peaches, cut into cubes
4 apricots, cut into halves
125g (4oz; 1 cup) white grapes
125g (4oz; 1 cup) cherries or black grapes

Wash the fruit thoroughly and prepare in a way that gives a variety of shapes and colours. Place the fruit in a serving bowl and pour over the grape juice.

Compote of apricots and peaches

225g (8oz; 2 cups) dried unsulphured apricots
4 fresh peaches
4 fresh apricots
50g (2oz; ½ cup) dried dates

Soak and cook the apricots in plenty of water to make extra juice. Allow to cool and add the fresh fruit and dates.

Rice porridge with prunes or hunza apricots

Use organic round-grain rice and cook gently with twice the normal quantity of water for at least 40 minutes until the rice becomes mushy.

Hunza apricots are available from healthfood stores or by mail order. Soak the apricots overnight and then cook them in plenty of water for 7 minutes. Once soaked, hunza apricots may also be eaten uncooked. Prepare prunes in the same way as the apricots. Buy prunes and apricots from healthfood stores and avoid the 'ready to eat – no need to soak' preparations.

Rice pancakes with apricot or plum purée

125g (4oz; 1 cup) rice flour
1 egg
1 tsp cream of tartar
250ml (½ pint; 1 cup) soya or coconut milk
FOR THE FILLING:
apricot or plum purée
honey

Place all the ingredients for the pancakes in a liquidizer and blend well, adding more liquid if necessary. Dry-fry on a griddle or in a heavy-based pan, pouring in sufficient batter to make just one pancake at a time. Cook until just golden on both sides.

Serve the pancakes warm, filled with apricot or plum purée, sweetened with honey if needed.

Waffles and drop scones may be made with this batter mixture using less liquid.

Rice flake muesli

Combine together rice flakes, chopped nuts and dried or fresh fruit. Serve with soya, rice or nut milk. You may also use grape juice or the juice left over from cooking prunes and apricots. Soak the rice flakes in the milk or juice for 5 to 10 minutes before serving.

Soups and starters

Cream of cannellini and almond soup

125g (4oz; ⅔ cup) cannellini beans, soaked and sprouted
75g (3oz; ¾ cup) ground almonds
1 litre (1¾ pints; 4 cups) stock or water
pinch of nutmeg
sea salt
25g (1oz; ¼ cup) flaked almonds

Cook the cannellini beans in a little of the stock. Add the ground almonds, allow to cool slightly and then blend in a liquidizer until smooth.

Return the liquid to the saucepan, add the remaining stock, salt and nutmeg and bring to the boil. Simmer for 4 to 5 minutes.

Serve hot or cold, garnished with flaked almonds.

Lettuce and tarragon soup

1 iceberg lettuce
750ml (1¼ pints; 3 cups) stock or water
150ml (5fl oz; ⅔ cup) soya yoghurt
1 tbsp chopped fresh tarragon
1 tbsp gram flour
1 tbsp walnut oil
sea salt
tarragon for garnishing

Shred the lettuce. Reserve a few shreds of lettuce for
garnishing, then place the rest in a saucepan with the gram
flour. Cover with some of the stock or water and bring to the
boil. Cook for 2 or 3 minutes. Blend the liquid in a liquidizer.

Pour the remaining stock into the saucepan and bring to
the boil. Add the liquidized ingredients and then stir in the
oil, soya yoghurt, nutmeg, tarragon and salt. Be careful not to
let the soup boil.

Serve with a garnishing of fresh tarragon and the reserved
lettuce shreds.

Spinach and egg-drop soup

225g (8oz) spinach, washed and chopped
1 litre (1¾ pints; 4 cups) chicken stock or water
2 eggs, lightly beaten
2 tsp miso or sea salt
½ tsp nutmeg

Place the spinach in a saucepan and cover with boiling water.
Cook for 3 to 4 minutes until tender. Allow the spinach to cool
slightly, then liquidize it to a purée. Return the purée to the
pan, add the stock or water, nutmeg and seasoning and
reheat. Remove from the heat and add the eggs, stirring until
they separate into strands.

Serve immediately.

Green pea soup

450g (1lb; 4 cups) fresh peas in their pods
1 cos lettuce
1 litre (1¾ pints; 4 cups) water
125ml (¼ pint; ½ cup) soya cream (optional)
sea salt

Shell the peas and reserve the pods. Take the outer leaves
from the lettuce and cook with the pods for 10 minutes in
some of the water. Allow them to cool a little and liquidize to
a purée. Pour the purée through a sieve and discard the pulp.

Bring the remaining water to the boil. Shred the lettuce
and add it to the water with the peas and salt and cook for 7
to 10 minutes. Liquidize and return to the pan with the pea
stock. Reheat and stir in the soya cream just before serving.

This soup may also be served with shredded smoked tofu
instead of soya cream.

Bean sprout and noodle soup

125g (4oz; 1 cup) mung bean sprouts
125g (4oz; 1 cup) lentil sprouts
125g (4oz; 1 cup) chickpea sprouts
1 litre (1¾ pints; 4 cups) boiling water
3 stalks Swiss chard, sliced
1–2 tsp miso or sea salt
50g (2oz; ½ cup) rice noodles

Chop the chickpea sprouts and place them in a large saucepan
with the lentil and mung bean sprouts. Cover them with
boiling water and cook for 10 to 15 minutes until tender.

Add the Swiss chard, miso and rice noodles and cook for a
further 7 to 10 minutes.

Stuffed vine leaves (dolmas)

225g (8oz) vine leaves
sprigs of tarragon to garnish
FOR THE FILLING:
125g (4oz; ½ cup) rice, cooked
125g (4oz; ⅔ cup) brown lentils, sprouted and cooked
25g (1oz; ¼ cup) fenugreek seeds, sprouted
125g (4oz; 1 cup) sunflower seeds, chopped
50g (2oz; ½ cup) raisins
nutmeg
sea salt

Mix together all the ingredients for the filling.

Spread out a vine leaf, smooth side down. Place a tablespoonful of the filling mixture in the centre of the bottom edge. Fold in the sides and roll the leaf up firmly to form a small sausage-shaped parcel. Repeat until all the vine leaves have been filled. There should be enough filling for approximately 20 dolmas.

Line the bottom of a shallow heavy-based saucepan, with the remaining vine leaves. Closely pack the dolmas into the saucepan. Add sufficient water to cover and bring to the boil. Simmer gently for 1 minute, leave to cool and then drain.

Serve garnished with sprigs of tarragon.

Spinach leaves may be used instead of vine leaves.

Spinach and tofu puffs

FOR THE CHOUX PASTRY:
125g (4oz; 1 cup) rice flour
125ml (¼ pint; ½ cup) water
2 eggs
4 tbsp sunflower oil or safflower oil
½ tsp sea salt
FOR THE FILLING:
275g (10oz; 1¼ cups) silken tofu
275g (10oz) spinach
2 tsp umeboshi purée or pinch of nutmeg
sea salt

Preheat the oven to 170°C (340°F), Gas Mark 4.

To make the choux pastry, place the oil, salt and water in a pan and bring to the boil. Slowly add the rice flour, beating with a wooden spoon to make a smooth dough. Allow the dough to cool slightly and gradually beat in the eggs to form a paste.

Using two spoons or an icing bag with a 2cm (¾in) diameter nozzle, drop eight mounds of dough on a baking sheet leaving room for the dough to expand. Bake for 20 to 25 minutes until the choux puffs are firm and golden. Use a serrated knife to slice the top off each puff. Leave to cool.

To make the filling, wash and drain the spinach and cook it in its own juices for 2 to 3 minutes until tender. Drain thoroughly and chop. Mix with the silken tofu and flavourings and beat to form a smooth paste.

Spoon the mixture into the choux puffs and replace the tops. Serve hot or cold.

This recipe may also be made up as a choux ring. Pipe the pastry onto the baking tray to form a 20cm (8in) diameter ring, leaving 10cm (4in) clear in the centre for the filling.

Almond and date stuffed peaches

2 large white peaches, peeled and halved
1 small iceberg lettuce, shredded
125g (4oz; 1 cup) chopped dates
125g (4oz; 1 cup) almonds, cut in half, lengthways
125g (4oz; ½ cup) silken tofu
sea salt
alfalfa sprouts for garnishing

Rinse the peach halves in salted water to prevent browning. Remove the stones and place the peaches with the hollow upwards on a bed of lettuce on individual plates.

Cream the tofu with the salt and put a spoonful in the centre of each peach. Arrange the dates and almonds on top with a few shreds of lettuce. Garnish with a sprinkling of alfalfa sprouts.

Chicken liver pâté

4 chicken livers
1 tbsp dripping
250ml (½ pint; 1 cup) thick white sauce
1 egg
1 tbsp freshly chopped tarragon
pinch of nutmeg
sea salt
FOR THE WHITE SAUCE:
1 tbsp rice flour
water
225ml (½ pint) soya, nut milk or stock

To make the white sauce, mix the rice flour with a little water.
Bring to the boil the liquid and stir in the rice flour. Cook
until the sauce thickens, stirring continuously.

Wash and trim the livers. Heat the dripping in a pan and
fry the livers gently until just cooked. Allow them to cool
slightly and place in a food processor with the white sauce
and the remaining ingredients. Blend until smooth. Spoon the
mixture into a pâté dish and refrigerate.

Stuffed artichokes

4 globe artichokes
450g (1lb; 4 cups) broad beans in their pods
125g (4oz; ½ cup) short-grain rice, cooked
2 tsp umeboshi plum purée

Preheat the oven to 160°C (325°F), Gas Mark 3.

To prepare the artichokes, cut off the stalks and trim the
bases so that they will sit flat. Use scissors to cut off the sharp
points of the leaves. Wash thoroughly and cook in plenty of
water for 40 minutes. Drain and set aside to cool.
Remove the beans from their pods and cook for 4 or 5
minutes until soft. Chop the beans roughly and mix with the
rice and umeboshi purée.

Pull out the soft inner leaves of the artichokes and scoop
out all the fibrous choke. Fill the cavity with the broad bean
mixture. Arrange in a covered ovenproof dish and bake in the
oven for 25 minutes. Serve hot.

Main meals

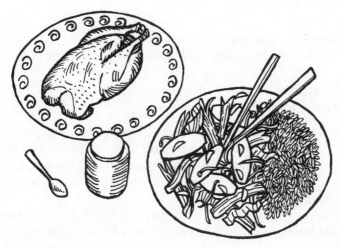

Pigeon with prunes

8 pigeon breasts
500ml (1 pint; 2 cups) stock or water
225g (8oz; 2 cups) cooked prunes
prune juice
2 tsp fresh tarragon, chopped
pinch of nutmeg
sea salt
2 tsp sago flour

Place the pigeon breasts in a flameproof casserole dish and add the stock, mixed with a little prune juice, and the tarragon, nutmeg and salt. Cover with a lid and cook over a gentle heat for 20 minutes. Lift out the pigeon breasts and place them on a serving dish to keep warm.

Mix the sago flour with some cold water and stir into the cooking stock until it thickens to make a sauce. Pour the sauce over the pigeon breasts and arrange the prunes around.

This dish may be served on a bed of rice with diced French beans and peas.

Turkey and apricot pilaff

675g (1½lb) turkey fillet
250ml (½ pint; 1 cup) stock or water
225g (8oz; 1 cup) wholemeal basmati rice
125g (4oz; 1 cup) dried unsulphured apricots, pre-soaked
50g (2oz; ½ cup) sultanas
½ tsp nutmeg
500ml (1 pint) salted water

Cut the turkey fillets into smaller pieces as required. Place them in a saucepan and cover with water or stock (you may use the soaking water from the apricots). Add the salt, nutmeg and fruit and cook for 20 minutes until the chicken is cooked through.

Meanwhile, cook the rice in 500ml (1 pint; 2 cups) of salted water for about 15 minutes until almost tender. Mix with the turkey and fruit and cook for a further 10 minutes until the rice is tender and has absorbed some of the juices.

Stir-fry duck with mangetout

450g (1lb) duckling breasts, cut into thin strips
225g (8oz; 2 cups) mangetout, topped and tailed
125g (4oz; 1 cup) bean sprouts
2 heads chicory, sliced
2 tsps honey
1 tbsp tamari soya sauce
50g (2oz; ½ cup) almonds, cut lengthways for garnishing

Heat a little water in a wok and add the strips of duck. Stir-fry for 5 minutes and then add the mangetout, bean sprouts and chicory. Cook for a further 7 to 10 minutes. Stir in the honey and soya sauce and garnish with almonds. Serve with brown rice.

Pot-roast pheasant/game bird

1 pheasant or other game bird
water or stock
nutmeg
salt

Preheat the oven to 190°C (375°F), Gas Mark 5.

Place the pheasant in a heavy-based casserole dish. Add enough boiling water or stock to half-cover the bird. Season with salt and nutmeg. Cover and cook for 1 to 1½ hours, reducing the temperature to 160°C (325°F), Gas Mark 3 after the first 15 minutes of cooking, until the meat is tender and is just beginning to fall away from the bone.

This is an excellent way of cooking game birds when the age and tenderness of the meat is unknown.

NB Some pheasants are fed on corn and this may affect some people. The same goes for corn-fed poultry.

Chicken with beetroot

4 chicken breasts
125ml (¼ pint; ½ cup) stock or water
675g (1½lb; 6 cups) beetroot, cooked and puréed
pinch of nutmeg
sea salt

Place the chicken breasts in a saucepan and cook with the stock and seasoning until tender. Serve hot on a bed of puréed beetroot.

Roast chicken with plum stuffing

1.6kg (3½lb) oven-ready free-range chicken
8 plums
FOR THE STUFFING:
125g (4oz; 1 cup) rice flakes
1 cup water
125g (4oz; 1 cup) sunflower seeds
4 red plums, stoned and chopped
1 egg or 1 tsp sago flour
sea salt

Preheat the oven to 190°C (375°F), Gas Mark 5.

To make the stuffing, soak the rice flakes in a cup of water for 10 minutes. Mix the stuffing ingredients together and bind with a beaten egg or sago flour. Stuff into the neck end of the chicken. Place the chicken in a roasting tin and roast for 20 minutes at 190° C. Reduce the oven temperature to 160° C (325°F), Gas Mark 3, and continue roasting for a further hour until the chicken is golden brown and tender.

Remove the chicken from the oven 15 minutes before the end of the cooking time. Strain off any excess fat and arrange the plums around the chicken. Return to the oven for the remaining cooking time.

Transfer the chicken to a serving dish and surround with the plums.

A purée of plums may be served as an accompaniment.

Vegetarian main meals

Artichoke and three bean casserole

6–8 artichoke hearts
175g (6oz; 1 cup) kidney beans, sprouted and cooked
175g (6oz; 1 cup) black-eyed beans, sprouted and cooked
175g (6oz; 1½ cups) fresh French beans, cut into thirds
500ml (1 pint) vegetable stock or water
½ tsp nutmeg
1 tbsp fresh tarragon or 2 tsp umeboshi purée
sea salt

Bring the water or stock to the boil and cook the French beans and artichoke hearts until tender. Add the remaining ingredients and flavouring and simmer for a further 10 to 15 minutes. Serve with rice.

Jerusalem artichokes may be used instead of globe artichokes.

Spinach and lentil flan

FOR THE RICE PASTRY:
175g (6oz; 1½ cups) rice flour
50g (2oz; ½ cup) soya or gram flour
½ cup sunflower oil
½ cup water
FOR THE FILLING:
175g (6oz; 1 cup) brown lentils, sprouted
350ml (12fl oz; 1½ cups) vegetable stock or water
275g (10oz) spinach
½ tsp ground fenugreek
sea salt
sunflower seeds

Preheat the oven to 160°C (325°F), Gas Mark 3.

Mix all the pastry ingredients together to form a dough. Unlike pastry made with wheat, this dough does not roll easily, so pat it down evenly into a well-oiled flan dish.

To make the filling bring the water or stock to the boil and add the lentils and salt. Cook for 20 to 25 minutes until the lentils form a purée.

Wash the spinach. Drain and cook it in its own juices in a covered pan. Drain, chop and mix with the lentils and ground fenugreek. Fill the flan case with the mixture and bake for 25 minutes.

Garnish with a sprinkling of sunflower seeds.

Tempeh or tofu stir-fry

275g (10oz; 1¼ cups) tempeh or tofu, cut into cubes
225g (8oz; 2 cups) mangetout, topped and tailed
225g (8oz; 2 cups) sliced green beans
125g (4oz; 1 cup) mung bean sprouts
2 heads chicory, sliced
1 tbsp Tamari soya sauce
2 tbsp sunflower oil
50g (2oz; ½ cup) almonds, cut lengthways, for garnishing

Heat a little water in a wok and cook the vegetables for two or three minutes. Add the tempeh and soya sauce and garnish with almonds.

Aduki bean burgers

225g (8oz; 1⅓ cups) aduki beans, sprouted and cooked
225g (8oz; 1⅓ cups) organic short-grain rice, cooked
125g (4oz; 1 cup) ground almonds
1 tbsp sago flour
1 tsp freshly chopped tarragon
sea salt

Mash all the ingredients together and shape into burgers or use a burger press. Grill for 4 to 5 minutes on each side under a low to moderate heat.

Extra quantities may be made up for freezing.

Spinach roulade with chickpea and salsify filling

FOR THE ROULADE:
1 litre (1¾ pints; 4 cups) spinach
sea salt
4 eggs separated
50g (2oz; ½ cup) rice flour
FOR THE FILLING:
225g (8oz; 1⅓ cups) chickpeas, sprouted and cooked
450g (1lb; 4 cups) salsify
sea salt

Preheat the oven to 170° C (340°F), Gas Mark 4.

Scrub the salsify and boil for 20 to 25 minutes, then peel and dice. Place in a food mixer with the chickpeas and salt and blend until smooth, adding some of the chickpea water to form a spreadable mixture.

Turn the cooked roulade out onto a large sheet of greaseproof paper and carefully peel off the lining paper. Spread with the filling and immediately roll it up, using the paper to help you. The roulade may be served hot or cold.

Line a 33 x 22cm (13in x 9in) swiss roll tin with greaseproof paper and brush it with oil.

Wash the spinach. Cut away and discard the stalks. Cook the spinach in its own juice for 4 or 5 minutes until tender. Allow to cool, then drain well and place in a food mixer with the egg yolks, rice flour and salt. Blend to form a smooth mixture.

Whisk the egg whites in a clean bowl until they form stiff peaks. Fold them into the spinach mixture and spread in the prepared swiss roll tin. Cook for 20 minutes until firm.

Vegetables and salads

Cherry and almond salad

350g (12oz; 3 cups) black cherries
1 nectarine
1 little gem or cos lettuce
125g (4oz; 1 cup) almonds, blanched
cold-pressed, unrefined safflower or sunflower oil

Wash and stone the cherries, reserving a few with stalks for garnishing. Wash the nectarine and cut it into small segments. Arrange the lettuce leaves around the edge of the plate and pile the fruit on top with the almonds. Sprinkle the salad with oil and garnish with the whole cherries.

Beetroot and chicory salad

4 heads of chicory
10 baby beetroots, cooked and skinned, or 2 large beets
cold-pressed safflower or sunflower oil

Discard the outer leaves of the chicory. Break off the inner leaves or cut through lengthways. Arrange the leaves on a serving dish and sprinkle them with oil. Cut the beetroots into strips or leave the baby beets whole and place on the top of the chicory just before serving.

Green bean salad

450g (1lb; 4 cups) French beans, cut in half
cold-pressed safflower or sunflower oil
sea salt
1 hard-boiled egg, sieved
175g (6oz; 1½ cups) alfalfa sprouts

Place the beans in a saucepan with a pinch of salt and enough boiling water to cover. Cook for 7 to 10 minutes until tender. Drain the beans well and toss in a little oil. Place them in the middle of a serving dish and sprinkle with the sieved egg. Arrange the alfalfa sprouts around the edge of the dish. The egg may be replaced with chopped walnuts.

Roasted Jerusalem artichokes

Preheat the oven to 170°C (340°F), Gas Mark 4.

Scrub and wash the artichokes and place them in a roasting pan. Pour over a little dripping from cooking game or poultry. Roast for about 45 minutes until golden.

Egg mayonnaise

2 egg yolks
2 tbsp wine vinegar
250ml (½ pint; 1 cup) safflower oil
½ tsp sea salt

Make sure the ingredients are at room temperature.

Place all the ingredients in a liquidizer except for the oil and blend for 1 minute. Remove the top from the liquidizer, turn to top speed and add a few drops of the oil at a time until the mixture thickens.

Tofu mayonnaise

225g (8oz; 1 cup) silken tofu
2 tbsp safflower oil
2 tbsp wine vinegar
sea salt to taste

Place all the ingredients in a liquidizer and blend until smooth.

Puddings and desserts

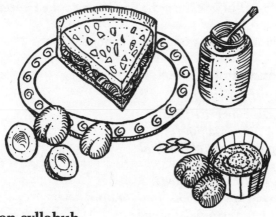

Damson syllabub

450g (1lb; 4 cups) damsons or plums
75g (3oz; ⅓ cup) unrefined beet sugar or honey
½ cup water
2 egg whites
1 tbsp sago flour

Wash the damsons. Place the sugar in a saucepan with the water and stir over a gentle heat until dissolved. Add the damsons, cover and simmer until soft. Mix the sago flour with a little cold water and stir into the damsons until the liquid thickens. Sieve the contents of the pan into a large bowl and allow to cool.

Beat the egg whites until white and fluffy but not dry. Gently fold into the damsons and spoon the mixture into individual glass bowls.

Chicory coffee ice cream

125g (4oz; ½ cup) honey
50ml (2fl oz; ¼ cup) almond oil
½ litre (1 pint; 2 cups) soya milk
2 eggs or soya egg substitute
2 tsp chicory coffee granules
125g (4oz; 1 cup) ground almonds for the topping

Beat the eggs and blend with the remaining ingredients.
Place the mixture in a shallow freezing tray and freeze until
just beginning to set. Remove from the freezer and whisk
until light and fluffy. Return the ice cream to the freezer
for 4 hours.

Serve with a topping of ground almonds.

Apricot and almond flan

FOR THE RICE PASTRY:
175g (6oz; 1½ cups) rice flour
50g (2oz; ½ cup) soya flour
125ml (¼ pint; ½ cup) almond oil
125ml (¼ pint; ½ cup) water
FOR THE APRICOT FILLING:
750g (1½lb; 6 cups) apricots, fresh or dried
125g (4oz; 1 cup) ground almonds
50g (2oz; ½ cup) flaked or chopped almonds
250ml (½ pint; 1 cup) water
1–2 tbsp honey (optional)

Preheat the oven to 150°C (300°F), Gas Mark 2.

Mix all the ingredients for the pastry together to form a
dough. Unlike pastry made with wheat, this dough does not
roll easily, so it is better to pat it down evenly straight into a
well-oiled flan dish.

Place a layer of ground almonds over the pastry base. Soak
the dried apricots for 4 to 6 hours, cut half of the apricots into
halves or slices, remove the stones and arrange on top of the
ground almonds.

Place the rest of the apricots in a saucepan with the water and honey. Bring to the boil and simmer until cooked. When cool, remove the stones and liquidize to a purée.

Pour the apricot purée into the pastry case and decorate the flan with the flaked almonds.

Bake for 35 minutes. Serve hot or cold.

Cakes and biscuits

Carob and coconut brownies

125g (4oz; 1 cup) carob powder
175g (6oz; 1½ cups) brown rice flour
125g (4oz; 1 cup) desiccated coconut
175g (6oz; 1½ cups) dates, soaked in 1 cup hot water
125ml (¼ pint; ½ cup) almond oil
2–4 tbsp honey
2 eggs, beaten

Preheat the oven to 160°C (325°F), Gas Mark 3.

Place all the ingredients in a bowl and mix well. Turn the mixture into a flat baking tin and bake for 45 minutes. Allow to cool in the tin before cutting into squares.

Sticky prune cake

125g (4oz; 1 cup) prunes
125g (4oz; 1 cup) rice flakes
1 cup water
3 free-range eggs
125ml (¼ pint; ½ cup) almond oil
1 tbsp honey
1 tsp cream of tartar
½ tsp bicarbonate of soda
FOR THE TOPPING:
50g (2oz; ½ cup) chopped almonds

Preheat the oven to 160°C (325°F), Gas Mark 3.
   Place the prunes in a saucepan with enough water to cover.
Simmer for 10 minutes until tender. Drain, remove the stones
and cut the flesh into small pieces. Whisk the eggs until thick
and stir in the prunes with the remaining ingredients.
   Pour the mixture into a lined, shallow cake tin
approximately 20cm (8in) square. Bake for 40 minutes until
firm to the touch.
   Decorate with the chopped almonds.

Rich fruit cake

275g (10oz; 2½ cups) rice flour
675g (1½lb; 6 cups) mixed organic dried fruit (eg raisins,
sultanas, currants, dried cherries, prunes, apricots)
125g (4oz; 1 cup) chopped almonds
6 tbsp oil (almond or sunflower)
6 free-range eggs or 2 cups apricots*
1 tsp nutmeg
1 tsp cream of tartar
½ tsp bicarbonate of soda
50–125g (2–4oz; ¼–½ cup) unrefined sugar or honey
*Cooked and puréed dried apricots may be used in this recipe as
an alternative to eggs. Use 1 tbsp of purée for one egg.

Preheat the oven to 150°C (300°F), Gas Mark 2.
   Line a 22cm (9in) cake tin with greaseproof paper.

Cream the oil with the sugar or honey and add the beaten eggs. Add the baking powder and nutmeg to the flour and fold into the mixture with the fruit and nuts.

Bake for 1½ to 2 hours. Leave to cool in the tin for 6 to 8 hours.

Chocolate almond cookies

225g (8oz; 2 cups) rice flour
125g (4oz; ½ cup) unrefined beet sugar
125ml (¼ pint; ½ cup) almond oil
25g (1oz; ¼ cup) cocoa powder
1 egg
50g (2oz; ½ cup) chopped almonds

Preheat the oven to 160°C (325°F), Gas Mark 3.

Mix the oil and sugar together and beat in the egg. Add the flour and cocoa powder and knead into a dough. Roll out on a floured board and cut into 5cm (2in) rounds. Place on a lined baking tray and top with chopped almonds.

Bake for 20 minutes. Allow to cool on the tray before transferring to a wire rack.

Cherry and coconut slices

125g (4oz; 1 cup) rice flakes, soaked in 1 cup water
2–4 tbsp honey
4 tbsp almond oil
2 eggs, beaten
50g (2oz; ½ cup) desiccated coconut
50g (2oz; ½ cup) dried cherries

Preheat the oven to 160°C (325°F), Gas Mark 3.

Mix all the ingredients together and turn into a well-oiled or lined 20cm (8in) baking tin. Bake for 25 to 30 minutes until firm to the touch.

Almond nougat

50g (2oz; ¼ cup) honey
175g (6oz; ¾ cup) light-coloured unrefined beet sugar
2 egg whites
125g (4oz; 1 cup) almonds, blanched and chopped
2 sheets rice paper

Line a swiss roll tin with rice paper. Place the honey and sugar in a heavy-based saucepan and heat until they form a bubbling syrup. Continue cooking until the syrup sets hard when a little is dropped into cold water.

Whisk the egg whites until stiff. Pour the hot syrup onto the egg whites, whisking all the time.

Place the mixture over a pan of hot water and continue whisking for 5 to 10 minutes until it becomes white and sticky and adheres to the inside of the bowl. Remove the mixture from the heat and whisk for another 2 or 3 minutes, gradually adding the nuts. The mixture should be elastic and chewy.

Pour the nougat into the swiss roll tin. Cover with another sheet of rice paper and weight it down overnight.

Rice bread

225g (8oz; 2 cups) rice flakes
water
50g (2oz; ½ cup) pulse flour (lentil, pea or soya)
2 eggs or 2 tsp sago flour
125g (4oz; 1 cup) ground almonds
1 tsp honey (optional)
1 tsp cream of tartar
½ tsp bicarbonate of soda
½ tsp sea salt

Preheat the oven to 160°C (325°F), Gas Mark 3.

Soak the rice flakes in water for 5 minutes, then mix with the beaten eggs or sago flour and remaining ingredients.

Turn the mixture into a 1lb lined loaf tin and cook for one hour until firm.

Raisin bun loaf

Follow the recipe for rice bread, adding 125g (4oz; 1 cup) raisins to the mixture.

Drinks and miscellaneous

Rice milk

50g (2oz; ¼ cup) organic short wholegrain rice
1 litre (1¾ pints; 4 cups) mineral water
1 tbsp unrefined, cold pressed safflower oil (optional)
1–2 tsps honey (optional)
1 vanilla pod (optional)

Wash the grains and place in a saucepan with the water. Bring to the boil with the vanilla pod and simmer gently for 1 hour. Cool slightly and then liquidize. Pour through a strainer and discard the pulp or use in other recipes. Add the sweetener, and more water if necessary. Add the safflower oil when completely cool. Keep refrigerated.

Soya milk (1)

75g (3oz; ¾ cup) soya flour (precooked variety)
1 litre (1¾ pints; 4 cups) mineral water
1 tbsp unrefined safflower oil (optional)
1–2 tsps honey (optional)

Liquidize all the ingredients together or mix with an egg whisk.

Soya milk (2)

175g (6oz; 1 cup) organic soya beans
1 litre (1¾ pints; 4 cups) water
1 vanilla pod
unrefined safflower oil
honey or grape juice (optional)

Soak and sprout the soya beans for four or five days, rinsing twice a day.

Place the sprouted beans in a saucepan with the water and vanilla pod. Bring to the boil and then simmer gently until tender. Remove the vanilla pod and liquidize. Pour through a strainer and add oil and honey to taste and extra water if necessary. Grape juice can also be used as a sweetener.

Honey egg-nog

(Serves 2)
500ml (1 pint; 2 cups) rice milk
1 large free-range egg
pinch of nutmeg
2 tsp honey
1 tbsp carob powder (optional)

Beat all the ingredients together and sprinkle with nutmeg. Carob powder can also be added if preferred.

Hot chocolate

(Serves 2)
2 tsps cocoa powder
½ litre (1 pint; 2 cups) rice or soya milk
2 tsp honey

Bring the milk to the boil and stir in the cocoa powder. Sweeten with honey.

Peach cocktail

2 ripe peaches or nectarines
½ litre (1 pint; 2 cups) grape juice
½ litre (1 pint; 2 cups) sparkling mineral water

Stone and peel the peaches and liquidize with the grape juice until smooth. Serve with equal parts of mineral water.

Almond and sunflower seed butters

Pre-soak the almonds or sunflower seeds overnight. Rinse and then liquidize, dropping a few nuts or seeds at a time onto the rotary blades. Add a pinch of salt to taste and a little of the corresponding cold-pressed oil to make a paste. Use the same day or freeze.

Day 4

The following foods can be eaten:

Cereals, grains and flour Buckwheat, buckwheat flour, buckwheat flakes and buckwheat pasta, sweet potato flour, chestnut flour, tapioca, amaranth, amaranth flour and amaranth pasta.

Meat, etc Beef, lamb, sheep's milk products, goats' milk products, cheese, butter, ghee, saltwater fish (cod, tuna, mackerel, eel, halibut, plaice, anchovy, sole, sardine, hake, haddock).

Nuts and seeds Hazelnuts and spread, walnuts, pecan nuts, chestnuts, poppy seeds, mustard seeds.

Sugars Maple syrup, apple and pear concentrate.

Drinks Sheep's milk, goats' milk, coffee, apple/pear juice, raspberry juice, raspberry leaf tea, rosehip tea, equisetum tea, lemon grass tea.

Vegetables The mustard family (Chinese leaves, cabbage, watercress, salad mustard and cress, mustard seed, cauliflower, broccoli, turnip, radish, daikon, horseradish, Brussels sprouts, kale, kohlrabi, swede), sweet potato, yam, dasheen, eddoes, sorrel, water chestnuts.

Herbs and spices The myrtle family (cloves, allspice), mustard seeds, lemon grass, capers, cider vinegar, raspberry vinegar.

Fruit   Pear, apple, loquat, quince, lychees, the rose family (strawberry, raspberry, blackberry, rosehip), pectin, rhubarb, guava.

Oils etc   Hazelnut oil, walnut oil. Cider vinegar, raspberry vinegar.

Breakfasts

Buckwheat and amaranth porridge
Buckwheat muesli
Amaranth and apple pancakes
Compote of strawberries and rhubarb
Fishcakes

Soups and starters

Cabbage and chestnut soup
Yam and watercress soup
Blue cheese and broccoli soup
Kohlrabi and goats' cheese soup
Oxtail soup
Pears with Stilton

Tuna fish roll
Sprout and chestnut dip
Amaranth ramekins
Lambs' liver with raspberries

Main meals

Fillet of beef with caper sauce
Pot-roast brisket of beef with horseradish sauce
Lamb or beef burgers
Buckwheat and walnut-coated herrings
Grilled halibut with anchovy butter
Fisherman's pie

Vegetarian main meals

Feta cheese and cabbage pie
Cauliflower cheese
Buckwheat pasta with broccoli and walnuts
Vegetable medley with buckwheat chappatis
Buckwheat chappatis
Amaranth and buckwheat nut loaf

Vegetables and salads

Fresh green salad
Fresh winter salad
Salad dressing
Mustard sauce
Pear and watercress salad
Baked red cabbage
Bubble and squeak nests

Puddings and desserts

Roly-poly fruit pudding
Tapioca milk pudding
Steamed apple pudding
Bramble mousse
Pears in raspberry sauce

Cakes and biscuits

Buckwheat and chestnut dropped scones
Apple and hazelnut muffins
Strawberry shortcake
Melting moments
Buckwheat and amaranth muesli bars

Drinks and miscellaneous

Strawberry yoghurt crush
Rosehip cordial
Hazelnut, walnut and pecan nut butters

Breakfast

Buckwheat and amaranth porridge

(Serves 2–3)
75g (3oz; ¾ cup) buckwheat flakes
50g (2oz; ⅓ cup) amaranth, soaked overnight
1 litre (1¾ pints; 4 cups) water
pinch of sea salt

Place the grains and flakes in a saucepan and add the water.
Bring to the boil and simmer gently, stirring occasionally, for
about 5 minutes until the amaranth is soft and the porridge
thickens.

Buckwheat muesli

225g (8oz; 2 cups) buckwheat flakes
50g (2oz; ½ cup) flaked or whole hazelnuts
50g (2oz; ½ cup) pecan nut pieces
fresh or dried fruit, chopped (apple, pear, raspberries, etc.)
rice syrup or maple syrup (optional)
sheep's milk, rice milk or raspberry, apple or pear juice

Mix the dry ingredients together. Cover with the milk or fruit juice and leave to soften for 5 to 7 minutes.

Amaranth and apple pancakes

1–2 dessert apples
FOR THE BATTER:
125g (4oz; 1 cup) amaranth flour
1 tsp bicarbonate of soda
125ml (¼ pint; ½ cup) water or sheep's milk
½ tsp allspice

Mix together the ingredients for the batter and beat well, adding more liquid if necessary to form a pouring consistency.

Peel and cut the apples into quarters and then into fine slices. Pour a little at a time of the pancake mixture onto a hot, non-stick griddle or pan to make individual pancakes. Cook for 1 minute and then add some slices of apple to the pancake so that the apple sinks in slightly. Turn and cook for a further minute on the other side.

Roll up the pancakes and serve.

Compote of strawberries and rhubarb

450g (1lb; 4 cups) strawberries
225g (8oz) rhubarb
½ cup water
2–3 tbsp concentrated apple juice

Wash the rhubarb stalks and cut them into chunks. Place them in a pan with the water and apple juice and cook until tender. Allow to cool. Wash the strawberries and cut any large ones in half. Mix with the rhubarb and serve.

Fish cakes

225g (8oz; 2 cups) sweet potato or yam, cooked and mashed
225g (8oz; 2 cups) cod or haddock, cooked
½ tsp mustard powder (optional)
sea salt

Preheat the oven to 160°C (325°F), Gas Mark 3.

Remove any bones from the fish, flake and mix in with the sweet potato and seasoning. Form into cakes and bake for 20 minutes.

Soups and starters

Cabbage and chestnut soup

175g (6oz; 1½ cups) dried chestnuts, soaked
1 small white cabbage, shredded
1 litre (1¾ pints; 4 cups) stock or water
sea salt

Cook the chestnuts with some of the water for 1 hour. Shred the cabbage and cook it with the chestnuts for 4 to 5 minutes until tender, reserving a little for garnishing.

Allow the cabbage and chestnuts to cool slightly and then liquidize to a purée. Return the purée to the pan, add the remaining stock and salt and reheat. Cook for 4 to 5 minutes. Add the remaining shredded cabbage and serve.

Yam and watercress soup

225g (8oz; 2 cups) yam, peeled and chopped
1 bunch of watercress
1 litre (1¾ pints; 4 cups) stock or water
½ tsp lemon grass
sea salt

Wash the watercress thoroughly, separate off the stalks and chop them. Bring a little of the water to the boil and add the yam and a pinch of salt. Cook until tender, adding the chopped watercress stalks towards the end of the cooking time. Allow to cool slightly and then liquidize until smooth.

Return the soup to the pan, add the remaining stock and lemon grass and bring to the boil. Simmer for 5 minutes, adding the watercress leaves during the last minute of cooking.

Blue cheese and broccoli soup

125g (4oz; 1 cup) yam or sweet potato, diced
275g (10oz; 2½ cups) broccoli, chopped
1 litre (1¾ pints; 4 cups) stock or water
125g (4oz; ½ cup) blue cheese, eg Stilton, Roquefort, Danish blue.

Cook the sweet potato in some of the liquid until almost tender. Add the broccoli and cook for a further 3 or 4 minutes. Cool slightly and liquidize to a purée.

Return the purée to the pan, add the remaining stock and bring to the boil. Simmer for 3 or 4 minutes and then remove from the heat. Stir in the crumbled cheese, allowing it to melt. Do not reheat the soup at this stage.

Kohlrabi and goats' cheese soup

450g (1lb; 4 cups) kohlrabi, diced
1 small sweet potato, diced
1 litre (1¾ pints; 4 cups) stock or water
½ tsp allspice
sea salt
125g (4oz; ½ cup) soft goats' cheese
salad cress for garnishing

Cook the kohlrabi and sweet potato in the stock or water until tender. Remove the rind from the goats' cheese and liquidize

with the vegetables and stock. Add the seasoning and reheat.
Serve with a sprinkling of chopped salad cress.

Oxtail soup

2 small oxtails from organically reared beef
2 small turnips, sliced
125g (4oz; 1 cup) swede, diced
1 litre (1¾ pints; 4 cups) water
1 tsp mustard seeds
sea salt
1 tbsp tapioca flour

Wash and dry the oxtails and cut them into joints. Put the
water in a saucepan and bring to the boil. Add the oxtail
joints, vegetables and seasoning and return to the boil.
Simmer gently for 3 hours or 1½ hours in a pressure cooker.

Take out the pieces of oxtail and cut the meat from the
bone. Return the meat to the soup and reheat. Mix the tapioca
flour with a little cold water and stir into the soup to thicken.

There may be a fair amount of fat on the soup which can
be removed with a basting pipette. Alternatively, allow the
soup to cool overnight and skim the fat from the top.

Pears with stilton

2 large pears
125g (4oz; ½ cup) crème fraîche
4 tbsp milk
50g (2oz; ¼ cup) Stilton cheese
1 tsp poppy seeds

Place the crème fraîche and milk in a saucepan over a gentle
heat. Crumble in the Stilton and stir until it is melted.
Remove from the heat and mix in the poppy seeds. Divide the
sauce between four small serving plates.

Cut the pears in half lengthways and remove the cores. Cut
each half into about eight segments, keeping the stalk end
intact if possible. Dip the pears in and out of salt water to
prevent them from browning. Arrange in a fan shape on top
of the cheese sauce.

Tuna fish roll

450g (1lb; 4 cups) sweet potato (pink-fleshed if possible), cooked
50g (2oz; ½ cup) tapioca flour
50g (2oz; ¼ cup) butter (optional)
225g (8oz; 1 cup) cooked tuna fish, flaked
50g (2oz; ¼ cup) crème fraîche or sheep's milk yoghurt
1 tbsp capers, chopped
25g (1oz; ¼ cup) horseradish, grated
1 tsp lemon grass
sea salt
mustard and cress or watercress for garnishing

Preheat the oven to 160°C (325°F), Gas Mark 3.

Mash the sweet potato, tapioca flour and butter until smooth. Line a swiss roll tin, measuring approximately 30 x 23 cm (12in x 9in), with greaseproof paper, and spread out the mixture to a thickness of about 1cm (½in). Bake in the oven for 20 minutes.

Mix the tuna fish with the remaining ingredients and spread over the potato mixture. Hold one end of the greaseproof paper and roll up the tuna and potato mixture. Leave to cool, then cut into slices with a sharp knife.

Serve on individual plates with a garnish of watercress or mustard and cress salad.

Sprout and chestnut dip

225g (8oz; 2 cups) Brussels sprouts
225g (8oz; 2 cups) cooked chestnuts
1 tsp ground lemon grass
sea salt

Cook the Brussels sprouts in a little water for 3 or 4 minutes until soft. Allow to cool slightly and liquidize with the chestnuts and seasoning. Blend to a smooth purée, adding some of the cooking water if necessary.

Allow the mixture to cool and serve as a dip with crudités. These can be pieces of raw swede, turnip or kohlrabi cut into matchsticks, radishes, cauliflower florets and stalks from Chinese leaves.

Amaranth ramekins

175g (6oz; 1 cup) amaranth
500ml (1 pint; 2 cups) stock or water
sea salt
50g (2oz; ½ cup) freshly grated Parmesan cheese
1 tsp tapioca flour
butter for greasing
125g (4oz; ½ cup) soft cheese (Brie or Camembert)

Preheat the oven to 170°C (340°F), Gas Mark 4.

Place the amaranth and stock in a pan with a pinch of salt and bring to the boil. Simmer until the amaranth is tender and all the water has been absorbed. Stir in the Parmesan cheese.

Grease four ramekin dishes and dust them with a little tapioca flour. Line the bottom and the sides with amaranth mixture and place a cube of soft cheese in the centre of each one. Cover the top with the remaining amaranth. Place the ramekins on a baking tray and bake for 20 to 25 minutes.

Lambs' liver with raspberries

225g (8oz) lambs' liver
sea salt
225g (8oz; 2 cups) raspberries
2 tbsp raspberry vinegar
2 tsp maple syrup
Chinese leaves for garnishing

Reserve 12 raspberries for garnishing and purée the remainder in a liquidizer. Strain and stir in the maple syrup and vinegar.

Cut the liver into thin strips, sprinkle with a little salt and grill for 3 or 4 minutes, turning until all sides are cooked.

Arrange the liver on four warmed plates and pour over the raspberry sauce. Garnish with Chinese leaves. If you did not eat any herbs from the mint family on Day 2, rosemary or sage could also be used as a garnish.

Main meals

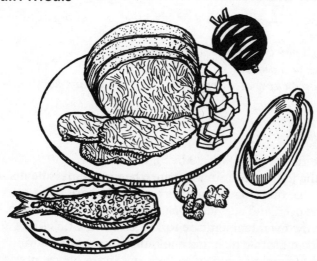

Fillet of beef with caper sauce

4 fillets of steak from organically reared beef
sea salt
FOR THE CAPER SAUCE:
3 tbsp capers
75g (3oz) anchovy fillets (in brine)
1 tsp ground lemon grass
1 cup sour cream
sea salt

To make the sauce, place all the ingredients in a liquidizer and blend until smooth.

Preheat the grill. Sprinkle the steaks with salt and grill for 3 to 5 minutes on each side according to preference. Spoon the sauce on top and serve immediately.

Pot-roast brisket of beef with horseradish sauce

1kg–1.5kg (2.2lb–3lb) brisket or silverside joint of organically reared beef
1 litre (1¾ pints; 4 cups) water or stock
1 tsp mustard seeds
450g (1lb; 4 cups) diced vegetables – swede, turnip, kohlrabi
sea salt
tapioca flour
horseradish sauce

Preheat the oven to 190°C (375°F), Gas Mark 5.

Put the joint of beef in an open, ovenproof casserole dish. Place in the oven for 20 minutes to seal. Remove the meat from the oven and add the stock, vegetables and seasoning. Reduce the oven temperature to 150°C (300°F), Gas Mark 2. Cover the casserole dish and cook for a further 2½ hours.

Place the meat on a serving dish and strain off the juices to make a gravy. Skim off any fat, reheat and stir in some tapioca flour, mixed with a little cold water. Keep stirring until the gravy thickens.

Serve with horseradish sauce (*see* below).

Horseradish sauce (1)

75g (3oz; ¾ cup) fresh horseradish, grated
1 small dessert apple, peeled and cored
175g (6oz; 1½ cups) turnip, diced
1 tsp ground lemon grass
½ tsp ground mustard seed
sea salt
2 tsps tapioca flour

Cook the apple and turnip in a little water until tender. Cool slightly and purée in a liquidizer with the seasoning. Return to the pan, reheat and use a little tapioca flour to thicken. Stir in the grated horseradish and serve.

Horseradish cream sauce (2)

75g (3oz; ¾ cup) fresh horseradish, grated
125g (4oz; ½ cup) double cream
1 tsp ground mustard
sea salt

Whip the cream until it forms soft peaks and fold in the grated horseradish, mustard and salt.

Lamb or beef burgers

175g (6oz) organic beef or lamb
*50g (2oz) ox liver or lambs' liver **or** 225g (8oz) beef or lamb*
125g (4oz; 1 cup) chestnut flour
1 tsp ground mustard (optional)
sea salt

Mince the meat and liver together. Mix in the chestnut flour and seasoning and shape into burgers. Grill for 4 to 5 minutes on each side.

Larger quantities can be made up for freezing.

Buckwheat and walnut-coated herrings

4 herrings
50g (2oz; ½ cup) buckwheat flakes
50g (2oz; ½ cup) walnuts, finely chopped
125g (4oz; ½ cup) sheep's yoghurt
1 tsp ground mustard seeds
25g (1oz; ⅛ cup) butter (optional)
sea salt or kelp

Wash and scale the herrings and cut off the heads. Slit the herrings open and remove the guts and backbones. Grill the herrings on both sides until almost cooked.

Mix together the ingredients for the topping and spread the mixture over one side of the herrings. Grill them for a further minute.

Grilled halibut with anchovy butter

4 halibut steaks
FOR THE ANCHOVY BUTTER:
75g (3oz) anchovy fillets
125g (4oz; ½ cup) unsalted butter

Preheat and grease the grill pan. Grill the halibut for 6 to 8 minutes until just cooked through. There should be no need to turn.

To prepare the butter rinse and dry the anchovies, then chop them finely and rub through a sieve. Beat the anchovy purée into the butter and form into pats. Serve with the halibut.

Halibut is in season from July to April but is available frozen throughout the year.

Fisherman's pie

450g (1lb; 4 cups) yam, cooked and mashed
450g (1lb) fillet of cod or similar fish
250ml (½ pint; 1 cup) sheep's or goats' milk
1 tbsp tapioca flour
sea salt

Preheat the oven to 160°C (325°F), Gas Mark 3.

Place the fish in a pan and cover with the milk and a pinch of salt. Bring to the boil and simmer very gently for 4 or 5 minutes until just cooked. Strain off the milk and place the fish in a pie dish.

Mix the flour with a little water and add it to the milk. Heat, stirring until the sauce thickens, and pour over the fish. Top with mashed yam and bake for 30 minutes.

Vegetarian main meals

Feta cheese and cabbage pie

FOR THE PASTRY CASE:
450g (1lb; 4 cups) sweet potato, baked, skinned and mashed
125g (4oz; ½ cup) butter
125g (4oz; 1 cup) tapioca flour
FOR THE FILLING:
225g (8oz; 2 cups) finely shredded cabbage
125g (4oz; ½ cup) feta cheese, thinly sliced

Preheat the oven to 150°C (300°F), Gas Mark 2.

Mix together the sweet potato, butter and tapioca flour and form into a dough. Take two thirds and press into a 23cm (9in) ovenproof flan dish.

Fill the pie with layers of thinly sliced feta cheese and finely shredded cabbage.

Roll out the remaining dough on a floured board, using tapioca flour to stop it sticking. Place it over the pie and trim to fit.

Bake for 45 minutes until the top is crisp.

Cauliflower cheese

1 large cauliflower
2 tbsp grated cheddar cheese
FOR THE CHEESE SAUCE:
50g (2oz; ½ cup) rice or tapioca flour
50g (2oz; ¼ cup) butter
250ml (½ pint; 1 cup) milk
250ml (½ pint; 1 cup) water
50g (2oz; ½ cup) rice or tapioca flour
½ tsp mustard powder
pinch of salt
125g (4oz; 1 cup) grated cheese

Wash and trim the cauliflower, discarding all but the very young leaves. Divide it into florets. Boil in a little salted water until tender. Retain the water and place the cauliflower in a flameproof dish.

Melt the butter in a pan over a gentle heat and stir in the flour for 2 to 3 minutes. Cook until the sauce thickens, stirring continuously. Cook for 2 to 3 minutes, allowing it to bubble but not to change colour. Remove the pan from the heat and gradually stir in the milk and cauliflower stock. Return the pan to the heat and add the salt and mustard and cook until the sauce thickens, stirring continuously. Add the grated cheese, stirring until it melts and pour over the cauliflower. Sprinkle with a little more cheese and place under the grill to brown.

Buckwheat pasta with broccoli and walnuts

225g (8oz; 4 cups) buckwheat spaghetti or pasta spirals
  (wheat-free)
675g (1½lb) broccoli
125g (4oz; 1 cup) walnuts, pre-soaked and chopped
2 tbsp walnut oil
sea salt
50g (2oz; ½ cup) freshly grated Parmesan cheese or walnuts
  (optional)

Cook the pasta in plenty of boiling, salted water until *al dente* (tender without being too soft). Drain and keep warm on a serving dish.

Cut the florets from the broccoli with a diagonal motion so that the stalks make oval shapes. (The rest of the stalks may be discarded or used in soup if you wish.) Add a sprinkling of salt and steam for 4 to 5 minutes until the florets turn a rich green, taking care not to overcook. Add the cooked broccoli and the walnuts to the pasta and spoon over the oil. Serve with grated walnuts or Parmesan cheese.

Vegetable medley with buckwheat chappatis

175g (6oz; 1½ cups) cauliflower and broccoli florets
8–10 radishes
175g (6oz; 1½ cups) swede, diced
1 kohlrabi, cut into matchsticks
1 sweet potato, sliced
125g (4oz; 1 cup) cabbage, shredded
sea salt
2–3 tbsp walnut or hazelnut oil
4 buckwheat chappatis (see below)

Prepare the vegetables and steam the swede and the sweet potato for 5 minutes. Add the cauliflower and broccoli florets, radishes, kohlrabi and cabbage and cook until just tender. Place on a serving dish, sprinkle with salt and spoon over the oil.

Roll up the chappatis and cut into 2cm (½in) scrolls and arrange on top of the vegetables.

Buckwheat chappatis

175g (6oz; 1½ cups) buckwheat flour
water

Mix the flour with water to make a firm dough. Break off small pieces and roll out into very thin rounds. Cook the chappatis in a dry frying pan until brown, then place them under a hot grill until they puff up.

Amaranth and buckwheat nut loaf

225g (8oz; 1 cup) amaranth, well cooked
175g (6oz; ¾ cup) buckwheat groats, cooked
125g (4oz; ½ cup) hard cheese, grated (optional)
125g (4oz; 1 cup) kohlrabi or swede, grated
1 dessert apple, grated
125g (4oz; 1 cup) walnuts, chopped
125g (4oz; 1 cup) hazelnuts, chopped
½ cup vegetable stock or water
1 tbsp tapioca flour
sea salt

Preheat the oven to 150°C (300°F), Gas Mark 2.

Mix all the ingredients together and pack into a well-oiled loaf tin. Cook for 40 to 45 minutes until firm.

Vegetables and salads

Fresh green salad

Mix together any of the following salad greens: Chinese leaves, watercress, mustard and cress, shredded cabbage and sorrel leaves. Serve with salad dressing (*see* below).

Fresh winter salad

Mix together any of the following: grated raw swede, grated kohlrabi, grated turnip, sliced radishes, water chestnuts, shredded white cabbage, chopped red dessert apple. Serve with salad dressing or mustard sauce (*see* below).

Salad dressing

125ml (¼ pint; ½ cup) cold-pressed walnut oil
125ml (¼ pint; ½ cup) cider vinegar
½ tsp ground mustard
1 tsp rice syrup
sea salt

Place the ingredients in a screw-top jar and shake well.

Mustard sauce

25g (1oz; ⅛ cup) butter
25g (1oz; ¼ cup) tapioca or rice flour
125ml (¼ pint; ½ cup) sheep's milk
1 tbsp cider vinegar (optional)
1 tsp ground mustard
sea salt

Melt the butter in a pan over a gentle heat and stir in the flour to make a roux. Cook for 2 to 3 minutes, allowing it to bubble but not to change colour. Remove from the heat and gradually stir in the milk. Return to the heat, add the mustard, vinegar and salt and stir until the sauce thickens.

Pear and watercress salad

4 ripe pears
salt water
1 bunch watercress, washed
½ tsp ground mustard seeds
2 tbsp cold-pressed walnut oil

Peel and quarter the pears and quickly immerse them in salt water to prevent browning. Arrange in a serving bowl with the watercress. Spoon over the oil and sprinkle with mustard seed.

Baked red cabbage

450g (1lb; 4 cups) red cabbage, shredded
2 eating apples or pears
salt water
2 tbsp cider vinegar (optional)
½ tsp allspice
½ tsp mustard seeds
4–5 cloves

Preheat the oven to 160°C (325°F), Gas Mark 3.

Peel the apples and cut them into small pieces. Immerse them quickly in salt water to prevent browning. Place the apple chunks in a casserole dish with the cabbage, vinegar, mustard seeds, allspice and cloves and bake for 1 hour.

Remove the cloves and serve hot or cold.

Bubble and squeak nests

450g (1lb; 4 cups) sweet potato or yam, grated
225g (8oz; 2 cups) cabbage, shredded
50g (2oz; ½ cup) amaranth or buckwheat flour
50g (2oz; ¼ cup) butter, soft
50g (2oz; ½ cup) grated cheese (optional)

Preheat the oven to 150°C (300°F), Gas Mark 2.

Mix the grated vegetables together and bind with the butter and flour. Divide into four mounds on a well-greased baking sheet and shape into nests. Top with grated cheese and bake for 35 minutes.

Puddings and desserts

Roly-poly fruit pudding

225g (8oz; 2 cups) amaranth flour
1 tbsp maple syrup
75g (3oz; ⅓ cup) butter
water or milk to mix
1 tsp bicarbonate of soda
FOR THE FILLING:
275g (10oz; 2½ cups) blackberries
1–2 tbsp maple syrup

Preheat the oven to 150°C (300°F), Gas Mark 2.

Sieve the flour and baking powder and place in a large bowl with the cream of tartar. Rub the butter into the flour and add the maple syrup and enough cold water to form a firm dough. Roll out between two sheets of greaseproof paper to approximately 30 x 23cm (12in x 9in), and 1cm (½in) thick. Cover with the raw blackberries and sprinkle on the maple syrup for the filling. Wet the edges of the pastry and roll it up like a swiss roll. Seal the edges firmly. Place in an ovenproof dish, cut three slits on the top and bake for 35 minutes.

Tapioca milk pudding

1 litre (1¾ pints; 4 cups) sheep's milk
75g (3oz; ¾ cup) tapioca flakes
1 tbsp maple syrup
knob of butter (optional)

Soak the tapioca in the milk for 1 hour.

Gently simmer the tapioca in the milk and add the maple syrup, stirring from time to time, until cooked. Serve with a spoonful of sugarless jam perhaps or, alternatively, with stewed or fresh fruit.

Steamed apple pudding

225g (8oz; 2 cups) sweet potato, baked, skinned, mashed
  and cooled
125g (4oz; 1 cup) buckwheat flour
2 large eating apples, peeled and chopped
125g (4oz; ½ cup) butter
1 tbsp concentrated apple juice
1 tsp ground cloves

Mix all the ingredients together. Butter a 1 litre (1¾ pints) bowl and pour in the mixture. Cover with a double layer of greaseproof paper.

Steam for 1 hour or for 30 minutes in a pressure cooker.

Bramble mousse

450g (1lb; 4 cups) blackberries
125ml (¼ pint; ½ cup) water
3 tbsp concentrated apple juice
15g (½oz) powdered gelatine
3 tbsp cold water
125ml (¼ pint; ½ cup) double cream (or sheep's yoghurt)

Thoroughly wash the blackberries and place in a pan with the water and the apple concentrate to sweeten. Bring to the boil and simmer for 5 minutes until soft.

Put the rest of the water in a bowl and sprinkle on the gelatine. Allow it to stand for 3 minutes, then stir it into the fruit. Rub the fruit through a sieve to remove the pips and make a purée. Allow the purée to cool. Whisk the cream until it forms soft peaks and fold into the purée before it sets.

Pears in raspberry sauce

4 firm but ripe pears, peeled
225g (8oz; 2 cups) raspberries
½ litre (1 pint; 2 cups) water
2–3 tbsp maple syrup

Put the water in a shallow pan and bring to the boil. Poach the pears for 10 to 12 minutes until they look slightly translucent but are still firm. Lift them out into a serving dish and cook the raspberries in the poaching water for 2 to 3 minutes. Pour the raspberries through a sieve to remove the pips, add the maple syrup to the juice and spoon this over the pears. Served with crème fraîche or live yoghurt.

Cakes and biscuits

Buckwheat and chestnut dropped scones

175g (6oz; 1½ cups) buckwheat flour
125g (4oz; 1 cup) chestnut flour
½ litre (1 pint; 2 cups) water

Mix together the flours and the water. Drop spoonfuls of the mixture onto a hot griddle; drop from the point of the spoon to ensure the scone has a good shape. Allow one dessertspoon of the mixture for each scone or one tablespoon if you want larger scones. When bubbles appear and the scone is just beginning to brown on the underside, turn with a flat spatula and cook on the other side.

Dropped scones are delicious with apple and pear spread, strawberry or raspberry sugarless jams, or served with yoghurt, pecan nuts and maple syrup.

Apple and hazelnut muffins

225g (8oz; 2 cups) sweet potato, baked, skinned, mashed
   and cooled
125g (4oz; 1 cup) buckwheat flour
125g (4oz; 1 cup) hazelnuts, shelled
1 large or 2 small eating apples, peeled and chopped
125g (4oz; ½ cup) butter
1 tbsp maple syrup (optional)
1 tsp allspice

Preheat the oven to 150°C (300°F), Gas Mark 2.

Remove the skins from the hazelnuts by placing in a grill pan and grilling lightly for 2 to 3 minutes. Rub the nuts between two sheets of kitchen paper or in a clean tea towel until the skins flake off. Chop the nuts.

Mix all the ingredients together and fill nine greased bun or muffin tins and bake for 15 to 20 minutes.

Strawberry shortcake

225g (8oz; 2 cups) amaranth flour
25g (1oz; ¼ cup) tapioca flour
125g (4oz; ½ cup) butter
125g (4oz; 1 cup) ground hazelnuts
FOR THE FILLING:
350g (12oz; 3 cups) strawberries
250ml (½ pint; 1 cup) whipping cream

Preheat the oven to 150°C (300°F), Gas Mark 2.

Rub the butter into the flours until the mixture resembles fine breadcrumbs. Add the nuts and knead into a firm dough, adding a little water to bind if necessary.

Grease or line two 20cm (8in) sandwich tins. Divide the dough into two and press well into each tin. Prick with a fork and bake for 15 minutes until it just begins to turn a light brown. Allow to cool before lifting out onto a wire rack.

Wash and hull the strawberries and cut them in half. Whisk the cream until it thickens and forms soft peaks. Reserve one half of the cream and mix the rest with half of the strawberries. Spread the mixture on one shortbread round, sandwich the other on the top and spread with the rest of the cream. Arrange the remaining strawberries on the top.

Melting moments

175g (6oz; 1½ cups) tapioca flour
125g (4oz; ½ cup) butter
25g (1oz; ¼ cup) chopped nuts for decoration (optional)

Preheat the oven to 150°C (300°F), Gas Mark 2.

Beat the flour and the butter together and place in a piping bag, fitted with a large star- or shell-shaped nozzle. Line a baking tray and pipe the mixture into shapes. Sprinkle some with chopped nuts. Bake for 20 to 40 minutes according to the size of the biscuits.

Buckwheat and amaranth muesli bars

125g (4oz; 1 cup) buckwheat flakes
125g (4oz; 1 cup) amaranth flour
125g (4oz; ½ cup) butter
2–3 tbsp rice syrup or maple syrup
50g (2oz; ½ cup) walnuts or pecan nuts, chopped
1 dessert apple, peeled and chopped

Preheat the oven to 150°C (300°F), Gas Mark 2.

Melt the butter and syrup in a pan over a low heat and mix in the remaining ingredients. Turn into a 18cm (7in) lined or greased tin and bake for 20 minutes.

Allow to cool before cutting and turning out.

Drinks and miscellaneous

Strawberry yoghurt crush

225g (8oz; 2 cups) strawberries, washed and hulled
225g (8oz; 1 cup) live sheep's yoghurt
2 tbsp maple syrup
250ml (½ pint; 1 cup) water or cold lemon grass tea
ice cubes (optional)

Liquidize the ingredients until smooth, adding the ice cubes
at the end.

Rosehip cordial

Gather well-ripened rosehips from the wild in early autumn
or from garden roses throughout the summer. Wash them
thoroughly and cut in half lengthways.

Place in a saucepan with enough water to float them and
bring to the boil. Simmer gently for 30 minutes and strain.
Sweeten with maple syrup, concentrated apple/pear juice or
rice syrup, according to taste, and use in drinks. Blackberries
or raspberries can also be added to the cordial.

Hazelnut, walnut or pecan nut butter

Pre-soak the nuts if you wish. Grind in a liquidizer, dropping
a few nuts at a time onto the rotary blades. Add a pinch of
salt to taste and a little of the corresponding nut oil to make a
paste. Spoon into a screw-top jar and store in the refrigerator.

CHAPTER 4

The Holistic Approach to Overcoming Food Intolerances

Health is not merely an absence of illness; in holistic terms it is a state of complete physical, mental and social wellbeing. We know that when we feel happy, peaceful and good about ourselves, our health improves. To overcome food allergy and intolerance problems, therefore, it can help if thought is given to all aspects of ourselves and our lives. We have a spirit, a mind and emotions, as well as a physical body. What we see on the physical body can reflect other parts of our being; so the more we can look, learn and heed the messages, the quicker our return to health will be. There are many forms of treatment available which may help you do this.

Acupuncture and acupressure

At the heart of oriental medicine is the concept that all life is an expression of energy. This energy manifests itself in different concentrations; the lightest concentration is found in the spiritual being, the 'Self', which connects us with the whole of the Universe, and the densest is in the physical body. In Chinese medicine, this energy, or *chi*, is said to flow through the body along meridian lines, rather like the current of a river, and if this energy becomes blocked or misdirected, health is impaired. With acupuncture, practitioners use fine sterile needles which they insert in specific points along the meridians. These balance the energies, thus treating the underlying cause of the symptoms. However, susceptible people can have an allergic response to the herb moxa, which is sometimes used by acupuncturists. Acupressure works on the same principles, but the practitioner uses his or her hands and fingertips instead of needles to activate the acupoints. This can be particularly useful for young children or for those averse to needles.

Alexander technique

This is an educational therapy which improves overall mental and physical wellbeing through changes in posture. It teaches you how to use your body properly, to maintain perfect balance and poise with minimum tension and energy and so avoid pain, strain and injury.

Aromatherapy

This is the modern name for the controlled use of plant essential oils in holistic treatments to improve health and prevent disease. These oils can be administered by massage, friction, inhalation, compresses or baths. However, allergic people can react to some of the oils, so take care when choosing them and do not overuse any one oil.

Bioresonance Therapy

Using the Bicom machine, this therapy regulates the electromagnetic field of the body and has been used successfully to stop allergic responses.

Chiropractic

This is a system of manipulation to treat disorders of the joints, particularly those of the spine.

Colonic Hydrotherapy

This is a form of water treatment for the elimination of toxic bowel waste. It provides exercise to the large bowel for the benefit of restoring proper absorption, health and wellbeing to the body.

Flower essences

In this therapy, remedies are made from the flowers of plants, bushes and trees and are used to treat the whole person. Dr Edward Bach, who developed the Bach flower remedies, viewed disease as stemming from 'a conflict between the Soul and the personality'. Essences are usually used to treat the body through treating the emotions, although some can be used for specific physical ailments.

Herbalism

This is the practice of using plants to treat and prevent disease. The treatment may be given in the form of fluid extracts, tinctures, tablets or teas. Herbs, like foods, need to be rotated in order to sustain a tolerance level.

Homoeopathy

This is a treatment based on the principle that 'like cures like'. It uses minute doses of animal, vegetable or mineral substances, which practitioners will prescribe in the form of tablets, pills, granules or powders. If a patient suffers a reaction to milk or sugar, these remedies can be obtained in a liquid form.

Kinesiology

This is a system of treatment based on the principle that muscle groups are related to specific parts of the body. A simple series of muscle tests are used to detect the energy blockages and imbalances which cause illness, and can then be used to ascertain what the body needs. In the hands of an experienced practitioner this method can also be a useful in detecting food allergies and intolerances.

Massage

This is a method of working on the whole body. Using hands and oils, creams or talcum powder, the therapist releases tension, relieves aches and pains, improves the circulation and lymphatic system and induces a relaxed state.

Nutritional therapy

This is a system of treatment and prevention which uses food and dietary supplements to enhance food assimilation, correct nutritional deficiencies, combat allergies and reduce toxic overload.

Osteopathy

This is a system of healing which deals with the structure of the body – bones, joints, ligaments, tendons, muscles and general connective tissue – in order to affect the functioning of the whole body. Practitioners use manipulation, massage and stretching techniques.

Radionics

This is a form of distant healing which works by determining and treating the fundamental causes that underlie the patient's symptoms.

Reflexology

This is a system of treatment that works on the principle that specific areas of the feet and hands correspond to parts of the body. By working with pressure on these areas, blockages in the energy pathways are released and encouraged to heal.

Shiatsu

This is a Chinese therapy whereby the practitioner uses hands and fingers, and sometimes knees and feet, to massage or apply firm pressure to the meridians to release and balance the flow of energy.

Spiritual healing

This is healing through the power of touch and thought. The healer acts as a channel for the transfer of healing energy to the patient.

T'ai Chi

This is an ancient Chinese martial art, now widely practised for its effectiveness as a form of callisthenics. It is suitable for people of all ages and can be tailored to all states of physical fitness, from the paraplegic to the professional athlete. The movements are slow, with the emphasis on control and balance. The very nature of the art stimulates blood circulation and benefits the internal organs, as well as loosening and limbering up joints and bringing about a state of mental relaxation to enable the natural healing processes to come to the fore.

Yoga

Yoga is a system of physical exercises believed to have originated before 4000 BC in India. According to its philosophy, its objective is to unite the 'self' with the higher consciousness through the harmonizing of body, mind and spirit. It improves both posture and breathing, benefits the circulatory, nervous and hormonal systems of the body, enhances flexibility and muscle tone and induces a state of relaxation.

Emotional healing

There are also many therapies for healing the emotions. You may, for example, feel angry, resentful, jealous or worried and whilst these are perfectly natural emotions, they can delay your return to health. Do not blame yourself or life situations for your emotions or negative thoughts but, instead, find a way to develop a calm and positive approach to life. The following therapies may help.

Counselling therapy

This can be very useful in helping people to explore their deeper emotions and negative thought patterns, which may be taking charge of their lives, and give them a different and a more positive perspective.

Hypnotherapy

This is a method of healing that induces a state of heightened receptivity during which the client/patient is open to new, positive ideas and therefore will be able to accept new solutions to their problems.

Neuro-linguistic Programming

This is based on the study of mental processes, language and body language of people and can help to heal emotional and psychological problems and can also be used for specific allergy and food intolerance treatment.

These are just some of the therapies that you may wish to investigate, as well as the self-help techniques explained in *The Elimination Diet Cookbook* for exercise, relaxation, meditation and visualization. However, above all else, there is the medicine of laughter. This has been described as 'intestinal jogging' and is a wonderful way of releasing tension. So, whatever it takes – funny films, books or tapes – make sure you laugh. The benefits can be enormous.

In conclusion

When you initially eliminated the foods to which you are allergic or intolerant, you probably noticed immediate results. However, whilst the benefits will not have been so apparent during this rotation diet, they will have been just as far-reaching. This diet is important because it will ensure that you do not become allergic or intolerant to any more foods. It is more than likely that this diet will aid your recovery even further by relieving any existing allergies or food intolerances. These books are about becoming your own expert. By following these diets, first to determine your allergies and food intolerances and then to rotate the foods that you are able to tolerate, you will give yourself the chance to experience the difference that diet can make to your wellbeing and state of mind. The more balanced you start to feel, the more your life will begin to run smoothly. More and more, you will intuitively know what you need to eat and when. You will then be able to look at yourself more clearly and honestly, ultimately finding the true meaning of inner happiness and fulfilment in life.

Philip developed hay fever at the age of two and was not a strong child. Constant infections kept him away from school. At 12 he developed severe depression, suffered from migraine symptoms, became very thin, occasionally hallucinated and eventually was not well enough to go to school at all. Philip was very ill for six years, but he then heard about elimination diets and food rotation. After the first week of eliminating the foods which he was reacting to, he was running about laughing and wanting to study. The headaches stopped and in the next two weeks all his various medicines were stopped. It took some time to regain good health, but Philip knew he was on the right track and he persisted. He persisted through a university course, cooking his own food and keeping to the principles of food rotation. He went backpacking across Canada, again carrying the special foods and finding places to cook them. He then took some postgraduate courses and settled into a job. Careful maintenance of a rotation diet has made all this possible as well as homoeopathic and radionic treatments. Philip has travelled across America, visited several European countries and travelled a lot in the United Kingdom. He has not let his diet get in the way of his life.

Appendix I

Weights and measures

Metric and Imperial measures have been given in this book. The recipes refer to Imperial pints as used in the UK and Australia which contain 20fl oz. The American pint, on the other hand, contains 16fl oz. Cups refer to the American 8fl oz measuring cup.

A teaspoon is standard at approximately 5ml. Tablespoons, however, do vary. The measures in this book refer to the UK standard, ie 17.7ml. The table below gives a conversion chart.

UK	American	Australian
17.7 ml	14.2 ml	20 ml
1 tablespoon	1 tablespoon	1 tablespoon
2 tablespoons	3 tablespoons	2 tablespoons
3½ tablespoons	4 tablespoons	3 tablespoons
4 tablespoons	5 tablespoons	3½ tablespoons

Appendix II

Food Ingredients

Foods containing wheat:
wheat flour
wheat bran
wheatmeal
wheat-based crispbreads
wheat biscuits
wheat breakfast cereals
    (All-bran, Weetabix, Puffed
    Wheat, muesli)
modified starch
baking powder
thickeners and binders
bakery products
some pumpernickel bread
cakes and cake mixes
batter mixes
spaghetti
macaroni and other pasta
pastry
mustard

also check the ingredients of the following:
baked beans
chocolate and other sweets
cocoa
instant coffee
imitation cream
custard
instant puddings
spreads and pastes
some other flours, eg rice flour
bean flours
buckwheat pasta
rye bread
sausages
beefburgers
hamburgers
corned beef
salami
luncheon meat
pâtés
foods coated in breadcrumbs or
    batter

canned soups
sauces
stock cubes
gravy
white sauce
soya sauce
chutneys
alcoholic drinks – whisky, most
   gins, lager, ale, beer, some wines
vitamin and mineral tablets

Foods containing milk and dairy products:

cows', goats' and sheeps' milk
condensed milk
dried milk
evaporated milk
skimmed and powdered milk
butter
buttermilk
cream
cheese including dishes cooked
   with cheese
whey
lactose
casinates
margarine (check whey on labels)
yoghurts
custards
biscuits
cakes
ice cream
foods cooked in batter
soups
sauces
sausages
prepared meats
most packets of convenience foods
some vitamin and mineral tablets

Homeopathic remedies can be
obtained in a liquid form free
from sucrose and lactose. Doctors
can contact manufacturers to find
pain-relieving medicines which
are milk free. Most tablets contain
lactose.

Foods and products containing corn:

adhesives
envelopes
stamps
stickers
lining of cans for vegetables
lining of paper plates and dishes
toothpaste
talcum powders
laundry starch
aspirin and other tablets
cough syrups
cornflower
sweetcorn
popcorn
biscuits
candies
instant coffee and tea
custard
instant whip puddings
ice cream
cornflakes
ales, beers, whisky and some
   wines
fizzy drinks
batters for frying
corn or maize oil
margarine containing maize oil
peanut butter
salad dressings
bleached white flour
powdered sugar
jam
milk in paper cartons
canned beans and peas
some brands of crisps
corn snacks
tortillas
gravy mixes and cubes
sausages
bacon
cured and tenderized ham
creamed soups
stuffing
glucose syrup and glucose in jams
monosodium glutamate (Chinese
   foods)
distilled vinegar
soya sauce
tomato sauce
salt-shakers in cafes
pie fillings
fruit juices
canned and frozen fruits
soya bean milks

boiled sweets
chewing gum
vitamin C is derived from corn

Foods containing eggs:
buns
croissants
Danish pastries
biscuits
cakes
flans
pastries and pies
salad dressings and salad cream
mayonnaise
some prepared salads
custard powder
ice creams
lemon curd
instant whips and processed
   cream preparations
egg white in meringues
macaroons
marshmallows
sorbets
consommé soups
frostings and royal icings
batter mixes made with egg
quiches
fishcakes
egg pasta
enriched alcoholic drinks
   (egg-nogs)
Many vaccines are grown on egg
   and may cause reactions

Foods which contain yeast:
breads
some biscuits
crispbreads
cakes and cake mixes
flour enriched with vitamins from
   yeast
food coated in breadcrumbs
some milk powders are fortified
   with vitamins from yeast (B
   complex vitamins)
mushrooms
truffles
cheese of all kinds
buttermilk and cottage cheese
vinegar and all convenience foods
   containing vinegar

gravy browning and similar
   extracts
yeast/beef extracts
stock cubes
fermented drinks – whisky, gin,
   wine, brandy, rum, vodka, beer,
   etc
malted products
cereals
sweets and chocolates
milk drinks which have been
   malted
citrus fruit juice (only home-
   squeezed are yeast free)
many B complex vitamin products
   are derived from yeast

Foods which contain sugar:
most alcoholic drinks
bakery products except
   stoneground wholemeal bread
instant coffee and tea
drinking chocolate
malted milk drinks
milk shakes
soft drinks and low-calorie drinks
fruit juices and squashes except
   pure fruit juices
most breakfast cereals
most precooked oven ready foods
milk products, eg baby milks
cream, whipped cream,
   ice cream
processed cheeses
some fruit yoghurts
many frozen and packaged foods
many jams
some honey may have sucrose
   added to it
sauces, eg tomato sauce
soya and other oriental sauces
mayonnaise
relishes
all sweets and candies
all tinned vegetables
fruits
soups
sauces
desserts are likely to contain sugar

Useful Addresses

AUSTRALIA

Allergie Association Austalia
PO Box 298
Ringwood
Victoria

Allergy Recognition and Management
PO Box 2
Sandy Bay
Tasmania 7005

Australian Natural Therapists Association
PO Box 308
Melrose Park
South Australia 5039
Tel 8297 9533
Fax 8297 0003

CANADA

AIA Allergy Information Association
3 Powburn Place
Weston
Ontario

IRELAND

Irish Allergy Association
PO Box 1067
Churchtown
Dublin

NEW ZEALAND

Allergy Awareness Association
PO Box 120701
Penrose
Auckland 6
New Zealand

New Zealand Natural Health Practitioners Accreditation Board
PO Box 37–491
Auckland
New Zealand
Tel 9 625 9966
Supported by 15 therapy organizations

UNITED KINGDOM

Action Against Allergy
43 The Downs
London SW20

Bioresonance Therapy
Regumed
3 Bryn Siriol
Gungrog Hill
Welshpool
Powys SY21 TN
Tel/Fax 01938 556800

British Digestive Foundation
3 St Andrew's Place
London NW1 4LB
Tel 0171 487 5332

British Homeopathic Association
27a Devonshire Street
London W1N 1RJ
Tel 0171 935 2163
Medically qualified homeopaths only

British Society for Nutritional Medicine
Stone House
9 Weymouth Street
London W1N 3FF
Tel 0171 436 8532

The General Council and Register of Naturopaths
6 Netherall Gardens
London NW3

The Institute for Optimum Nutrition
Blades Court
Deodar Road
London SW15 2NU

Society for the Promotion of Nutritional Therapy (SPNT)
PO Box 47
Heathfields
East Sussex TN21 8ZX
USA

Allergy Foundation of America
801 Second Avenue
New York 10017

American Association of Naturopathic Physicians
2800 East Madison Street
Suite 200
Seattle
Washington 98112
or
PO Box 20386
Seattle
Washington 98102
Tel 206 323 7610
Fax 206 323 7612

International Academy od Enviromental Medicine
Prairie Village
Kansas
Tel 913 642 6062

Internal Academy of Nutrition and Preventative Medicine
PO Box 5832
Lincoln
Nebraska 68505
Tel 402 467 2716

Further Reading

Bloomfield, B, *The Mystique of Healing*, Skilton & Shaw, Edinburgh, 1984

Brostoff, Dr J and Gamlin, L, *Food Allergy and Intolerance*, Bloomsbury, London, 1989

Budd, Martin, *Low Blood Sugar*, Thorsons, London, 1995

Carter, Jill, and Alison Edwards, *The Elimination Diet Cookbook*, Element Books, Shaftesbury, England, 1997

Davies, Gwynne, *Overcoming Food Allergies*, Ashgrove, Bath, England, 1985

Davies, Dr S and Stewart, Dr A, *Nutritional Medicine*, Pan Books, London, 1987

Dong, Dr, *New Hope for the Arthritic*, Granada Press, St Albans, England, 1980

Erasmus, Udo, *Fats that Heal, Fats that Kill*, Alive Books, Burnaby, Canada, 1993

Galland, Dr L, *Allergy Prevention for Kids*, Bloomsbury, London, 1989

Lewith, Dr G, Kenyon, Dr J and Dowson, Dr D, *Allergy and Intolerance*, Merlin Press, London, 1992

Mackarness, R, *Chemical Victims*, Pan, London, 1980

Mackarness, R, *Not all in the Mind*, Pan, London, 1976

Mansfield, Dr P and Munro, Dr J, *Chemical Children*, Century Paperbacks, London, 1987

Mental and Elemental Nutrients, Brain Bio Centre, Princetown, New Jersey, USA, 1975

Needes, R, *You Don't Have To Feel Unwell*, Gateway, Bath, England, 1984

Randolph, T and Moss, R, *Allergies: Your Hidden Enemy*, Turnstone, Wellingborough, England, 1981

Rapp, Doris J, *Allergies and the Hyperactive Child*, Sterling Publishing, New York, 1988

General Index

Index of Foods and Recipes

The day reference indicates the day on which the food may be eaten. Recipes are given in italic where the food is an important ingredient.

flageolet beans   (pea family) *day 3*
flax seed oil – linseed 15, *day 2*
French beans   (pea family) *day 3*
    artichoke and three bean casserole 92
    green bean salad 96
French dressing   see *salad dressing*
fruit sugar *day 2*

game   (bird family) *day 3*
    game stock 20
garlic   (lily family) *day 2*
ghee – clarified butter 15, *day 4*
ginger   (ginger family) *day 2*
    spiced pumpkin and ginger soup 59
    ginger fork biscuits 75
goose   (bird family) *day 3*
grapes   (grape family) *day 3*
grapefruit   (citrus family) *day 1*
    grapefruit and orange salad 27
    papaya and grapefruit salad 32
green leaf tea   (tea family) *day 1*
green banana flour *day 2*
    green banana and oatmeal scones 73
    ginger fork biscuits 75
grouse   (bird family) *day 3*
    pot roast pheasant/game bird 90
guava   (myrtle family) *day 4*
gooseberry   (gooseberry family) *day 2*
    gooseberry crumble 71

haddock, hake   (saltwater fish
    family) *day 4*
    fish cakes 110
halibut   (saltwater fish family) *day 4*
    *grilled halibut with anchovy
        butter* 118
hare   (rabbit family) *day 1*
    rabbit/ hot pot 35
haricot beans   (pea family) *day 3*
hazelnut   (birch family) *day 4*
    apple and hazelnut muffins 128
    *hazelnut, walnut and pecan nut
        butters* 130
hemp seeds/oil   (moraceae family)
    20, *day 2*
    hemp seed bread 73
    hemp seed milk 77
    hemp seed butter 78
herrings   (saltwater fish family) *day 4*
    *buckwheat and walnut coated
        herrings* 117
hibiscus   (mallow family) *day 2*
honey *day 3*
horseradish   (mustard family) *day 4*
    sauce 116, 117
Hunza apricots *day 3*
    with rice porridge 82

juniper   (conifer family) *day 2*
    roast pork/wild boar with juniper 63

kamut   (grass family) 15, *day 1*
    millet and kamut porridge 28
kelp – salt substitute (seaweed family)
    15, *day 1*
kidney beans   (pea family) *day 3*
    artichoke and three bean casserole 92
kiwi fruit – Chinese gooseberry
    (dillenia family) *day 2*
kohlrabi   (mustard family) *day 4*
    kohlrabi and goats' cheese soup 111
kombu   (seaweed family) *day 1*

lamb   (beef family) *day 4*
    lambs' liver with raspberries 114
    lamb burgers 117
leek   (lily family) *day 2*
lemon   (citrus family) *day 1*
    salad dressing 40
    lemon and orange barley water 50
    lemon and elderflower cordial 51
lemon balm   (mint family) *day 2*
lemon grass   (grass family) *day 4*
lemon verbena   (verbenaceae family)
    day 2
lentils   (pea family) *day 3*
    spinach and lentil flan 93
    sprouting 20–21
lettuce   (aster family) *day 3*
    lettuce and tarragon soup 84
lima beans   (pea family) *day 3*
linseeds – flax seeds *day 2*
liver   *chicken liver pate* 88
    lambs' liver with raspberries 114
    pigs' liver and onions 63
lobster   (crustacean family) *day 1*
loquat   (apple family) *day 4*
lovage   (parsley family) *day 1*
    cream of celery and lovage soup 31
lychees   (soapberry family) *day 4*

macadamia nuts   (proteacea family)
    day 2
    *grilled pineapple and macadamia
        nuts* 71
mace   (nutmeg family) *day 3*
mackerel   (saltwater fish family)
    day 4
maize   see *corn*
malt   barley *day 1*
mangetout   (pea family) *day 3*
    stir fry duck with mangetout 90
mango   (cashew family) *day 1*
    *grilled trout fillets with tropical
        fruit* 35
maple – syrup (maple family) *day 4*